THE

BEST

OF

LIFE

SILESIA BROWN

DEDICATION

This book is dedicated to my Lord and Saviour Jesus, who is my strength, my guidance, my model and my rock. Without Him I would not be where and who I am today.

The best of life

ACKNOWLEDGEMENTS

I would like to say thanks to my family, Martin my husband, our son Joao-Lucas and our daughters Mia and Maisie. They are my life, my joy and my safe harbour.

I would also like to thank early readers Jaqueline Steer, Perrim Smith, Ana Flávia Smith and Helen Lee for your support and encouragement. A big thanks to Adele Hooper for editing the book in English and Maria Eunice Gennari for editing in Portuguese. Thanks to Candice J Mitchell for doing the copy-editing and proofreading. Thanks to Carlos Alberto Silva (Queco) for creating the book cover. Thanks to Ana Carolina Cardoso for all the help and advice. Thanks to all my friends that helped me to choose my cover and to promote the book. And last, but not least, thanks to Sue Sundstrom for your accountability, coaching and for believing in me.

The best of life

CONTENTS

The best of life

INTRODUCTION

I would like to invite you to go on a journey with me which will take you through my life experiences and show you how I am walking towards a fullness of life with God, how I have learnt to understand His will, to accept it, and to trust God. It wasn't easy to open myself up to write this book, but I am doing it in obedience, because I feel strongly in my heart that God wants me to do it to bless you and others around you.

I know that, nowadays, we have so many books about purpose, plan, and life coaching to teach us how to live a fulfilled live. There are people who are highly trained to give you their best and I personally think that they are doing a great job as they have helped thousands and thousands of people around the world.

There is something I would like to make clear; I am not a trained and qualified life coach. I am an ordinary lady, wife, and mum of three who absolutely loves God and has been learning how to trust Him completely, to be sensitive to His voice guiding me through my life. God asked me to write this book and if you are reading it now, it is because He wants to bless you through my life story and if you know someone who can be blessed through it too, please recommend this book to that person.

I really hope you are going to be blessed reading this book as much as I was writing it.

PART I

SEARCHING
FOR MY PURPOSE

My life before coming to the UK

The best of life

CHAPTER 1

WHO DOES PLAN OUR LIVES?

A few years ago, a friend recommended an article to me written by an author who believes that God does not plan our lives. He believes that we can live as we please and we can make the decisions and choices we desire, and we are responsible for our own destiny. Honestly, I cannot say much more about the article because, in fact, I could not finish it because at that time I was experiencing something different in my life. Now, a few years later, I have begun to think about my life and what that article meant to me.

God has given us free will and with that comes the freedom to make plans, make choices and live our lives as we wish. The results of our choices will depend on how wise we are in our decisions and how effective we are in putting them into action. When we use free will to make our own plans and choices, we are often motivated by the desire to be respected and accepted by everyone around us.

On the other hand, there is the option of dependency on the Lord. This happens when we fully place our faith and trust in God, believing that He has the best for us, that He has control of our lives and of all the situations around us. In this case, we put ourselves in God's hands and let Him make plans for us and we make our decisions according to His plans for our lives.

The Word of God says in Jeremiah 1:5

> *"Before I formed you in the womb, I knew you; before you were born, I set you apart; I appointed you as a prophet to the nations."*

And it also says in Jeremiah 29:11

> *"For I know the plans I have for you,"* declares the Lord, *"plans to prosper and not to harm you, plans to give you hope and a future."*

God knows us deeply and loves us. He can see and hear our hearts. He has a different plan prepared for each one of us according to His purpose for me and for you, respecting each person's individuality.

When I personally decided to choose God's way, I had to take some steps towards the search for my purpose to ensure it was established on God's plan for my life. Bear in mind that this choice is available for your life too. I will tell you about my experience throughout this book but before I do that, I will summarise the steps I took to help you understand the whole picture.

Step One, I accepted Jesus as the Lord and Saviour of my life. After that, I left the old me behind and started to form a better version of myself. This is a long process, and it will go on until our purpose here on earth is fulfilled. In another words, this is a process which goes on as I grow in stature and wisdom before God and men or as I grow in maturity and intimacy with our God.

The decision to accept Jesus is individual and it is up to each person. Jesus will not force us to make this decision or break into our hearts. He is kind and respects our decisions.

The bible says in Revelation 3:20 *"Here I am! I stand at the door and knock. If anyone hears my voice and opens the door, I will come in and eat with that person, and they with me."*

Step Two, I continually aspire to be sensitive to God's voice, so that I can hear his guidance to let myself be carried away by the movement of the Holy Spirit blowing like a morning breeze on my face, in a light and gentle way. After all, our Lord is gentle and has the best for our lives.

Step Three, I motivate myself to leave my comfort zone and tranquillity to follow in the direction that the Lord is taking me. Although the Spirit's breath is light and smooth, it does not mean that our journeys will be the same. After all, when we enter the boat with Jesus, there will always be resistance and storms. But with Jesus on the boat, it is for sure that we will arrive on the other side safe despite the gallows and brutality of the resistance that surrounds us. With Jesus on the boat, we will feel safe and never forsaken.

Each one of us is free to make our own choice, but do not forget that with freedom comes responsibility for our own decisions.

With that in mind, I made my choice and decided to have Jesus in my life. I have been practicing these 3 steps in my life and as a result, I have harvested the best of the earth. Throughout my testimony I will expose to you the most important and remarkable details of my life so that you can understand how much the Lord has blessed me and taught me so that I can become the best version of myself and fulfil his purpose for my life.

So, I began to think about my life from birth, what my mother told me and the experiences I had throughout my existence until now. Each of my memories is precious, each one of them has got its own meaning and purpose. I cannot remember all of them of course, some of them got lost over the years. This can happen when a memory is not as important as the ones that were marked in our lives. I like comparing our mind to a computer. When it gets to its full memory capacity, it needs to have some files deleted to create space in its memory to be able to receive new information or it can also have its memory capacity enlarged. Likewise, we forget less important memories to make room for new and more important memories for the new season we are living in. On the other hand, the most striking memories are there, registered and are part of our growth as individuals, helping us to become more mature.

When I went back in my life, I found myself in the presence of my Father, not my biological father, but in the presence of the one who is known as the Creator, the one who is called I Am. Our Father in heaven. Oh yes, I could see my life as a book in my mind when I closed my eyes. I could even separate it into parts and called each one of them a chapter of the great plan that God has prepared for my life. It was so strong that I had to share it, I could not keep it just for myself. I felt I had to do something about it, so I started writing about it.

We never know, maybe there is someone out there who is going to be blessed with my story. I hope you are as blessed reading this book as I have been by writing it.

CHAPTER 2

LISTENING TO GOD

I was born in Brazil in a medium-sized city called Patos de Minas, in Minas Gerais state. It is in the south east of Brazil. When I left my city in 1987, at 20 years old, there was a population of around 80,000 people. It was and still is a lovely city, although the population has increased by more than 40,000. When I left my homeland, my father was a well-known man there, he was the family provider, and he was able to offer a good life to his family. I was privately educated in two of the best schools in the city. But it was not always like that, my mother and father came from a very poor background. My mother was raised on a farm, her father was a farm worker. She moved to the city after her 16th birthday, where she eventually worked as a housekeeper and my father was a bricklayer. They got married when my mother was 25 and my father was 18. Since my mother's first pregnancy, my parents really wanted a girl. I am the third of their four biological children and the only girl. It was not easy growing up in a house with only brothers. My dear cousin, Suely, became my sister when I was 13 and she was 9, after her mother died. My aunt was my father's sister. I was happy to share my room with Suely. My three brothers

(Cleber, Eder and Clenio) were typical boys. After school each day, they spent time with friends; playing in the street, riding bicycles, climbing trees, having fun, and enjoyed life. And they had a lovely childhood, full of fun. After I turned 5 my parents' financial position improved and we were not as poor anymore.

I cannot say my childhood was also full of fun. I was overprotected as the only girl and I could not go out and play with friends outside our home or go to their homes. I could have friends in my house, just girls, but they just started coming over after I was 13, before that, I was alone. I had my mother with me at home, but she was always busy with housework. She liked her house perfectly clean, and I could not help her. My father wanted to raise me like a princess, my mother used to do everything for me. Our family lifestyle was my father's choice. Despite being a lot younger than my mum he had a very strong personality, and he was the boss. None of my cousins and friends at school lived with these rules, and it used to make me feel different. I was not allowed to leave home without the supervision and protection of a responsible person. That person was one of my parents or my older brother, he is only 2 1/2 years older than me, but he was a very sensible boy and he used to take good care of me as my parents trusted him. I was taken to school and collected from there every day by one of these three members of my family.

Once I was at home, I had to entertain myself watching TV, reading books, or doing school homework. They meant well, they wanted to protect me, keep me safe and this is how they showed me how much they loved me and how much I was wanted in their lives.

My parents really wanted a baby girl. My name was chosen when my mother was expecting my older brother. At that time, the sex of the child was a surprise as they did not have scans in our city yet. After my eldest brother was born, they had to go through another pregnancy as their second child was another boy. I came after their third pregnancy. They finally saw me for the first time in September 1966. A year later she had another boy. My mother gave birth to all four of her children at home with the help of a midwife, bear in mind that in the 60s they did not have the same level of education as they have nowadays. The midwives were ordinary ladies who learnt from another lady how to deliver babies. My father was an old-fashioned man, and he would not take my mother to the hospital. He would not allow her to be examined by a male doctor and at that time they did not have a female doctor in my town. My parents were very poor, my mother stayed home with the children and my father was a builder, which was not a well-paid job in Brazil. My mum was so happy to finally hold a little girl in her arms that she did something amazing, which she told me about at my hen party when I was 37, something I am going to tell you about later, so keep that in mind. What I can say now is that things in my life started to make sense in my mind and to stick together like a big puzzle. I used to be very confused, wondering why I have been so blessed and I feel sometimes that I have been given more in life than my brothers and cousin. What my mum told me explains a lot, but not everything, I know now after having grown up a lot in maturity that what she did was the beginning of God's great plan for me. I believe that God has a purpose for each one of us and what I have today, and the life I live today is God's purpose for me. It has its difficult moments despite living in the United Kingdom, a country where the quality of life is much better that of the life in Brazil.

I finally understood why I was guided by God from the age of 6, when I began to hear God's voice and be given direction about what he expected me to do and what he was planning for my life. I have had several experiences over the years and my intention is to share them all with you in this book. I would like you to read and learn something about God's plans for our lives through my life and my experience. It is my first time writing a book and English is not my first language. My purpose in not to write a best seller, I just really want to share with as many people as possible what God has done in my life.

GOD STARTED TALKING TO ME

When I was 6 years old, my parent's financial position was just starting to improve, but we were still living in a poor, very small home, with just two bedrooms. I will never forget this house, it was a very special place for me because it was there that I started to hear God's voice. Yes, that is what I said, I started to hear God's voice giving me directions in my life when I was just 6 years old. God told me to go to church. My family did not used to go to church at that time, so I had no real model in my life to encourage me to go to church and start learning about God. No one ever told me about God, my mum was a wonderful mum, but she used to be very busy looking after her children, husband, and home. Everything around the house was done by hand, including washing clothes. There was no washing machine yet.

The experience I had with church, in general, was very limited. I used to live a few yards from the main Catholic Church in my town, it was called Cathedral. On special occasions, mainly Good Friday, there would be a procession on the street, followed by a service outside the church with a play about Jesus Christ's crucifixion story. It was very popular and because of the number of people gathered it, had to be done outside the church so everybody could watch it. The church entrance was big and raised, and used to be turned into a stage. Also, there was a good car park just outside and the main square across the car park. So, it was a good spot to accommodate all the church-going people and those people like my mum and her children who just used to go to the Good Friday service outside the church. My parents baptised their four children too and we all had our first communion preparation course when each one of us reached the age of 9 years old. It was a very respected and popular tradition in my city for families to gather to watch their children take their first communion during a special service organised by the church and the school. During one Good Friday service, before I was 5 years old, the church decided that it would be more effective to tie an actor on the cross to show people the horrible death Jesus went through. When the cross was raised from the floor, my mum's reaction was very scary, very negative, she didn't see it like the producers saw it. She felt very hurt at seeing an ordinary young man playing Jesus and being raised while tied to the cross. My mum held my and my little brother's hand and called my two other brothers to leave the service to return home. She was very cross and said to my dad, "How dare a sinner pretend to be Jesus and be put on the cross like that." After that she did not go back to the Good Friday service anymore. She just used to take us to watch some of the street procession which passed nearby our home, and I quite enjoyed it.

One day, when I was 6 years old, I heard God telling me to go to church.

So, I went to my mum and I asked her to take me to church because I really wanted to go. My dad would not allow her to go on a regular basis, but he told my older brother, who was 8 years old, to take me and the other two brothers to a Sunday morning service for children at the Catholic Church around the corner from my home. It was a big adventure for me, I used to love it, it was so enjoyable, so rewarding. So, I carried on going to the Catholic Church service until my early twenties.

Let us go back to the verse in Jeremiah 1:5:

> *"Before I formed you in the womb, I knew you; before you were born, I set you apart; I appointed you as a prophet to the nations."*

God knew me deeply and so He knew what I needed to do, step by step, to walk in line with his will and to focus on my journey to avoid taking a wrong turn which would delay His plans in my life, but for sure His plans cannot be frustrated. God's plans can be delayed but they cannot be frustrated.

Job 42:2

> *"I know that you can do all things; no purpose of yours can be thwarted."*

GOD TELLS ME: I WILL TAKE YOU ACROSS THE OCEAN

When I was 11 years old, I went to a private Catholic school for girls to start my secondary school education. It was just across from the Catholic Church I used to go to. I used to love it there, I had some good friends and in the year that I started going to that school there were a handful of boys, the school was starting to open up to them. Overall, I was a very good student, very dedicated and responsible.

In Brazil we have school in the morning from 7am until 11.30am. And then after lunch from 1pm until 5.30pm another group of children will attend. So, in my time there, the children from 11 to 14 years old used to go to the afternoon session and the young people from 15 to 18 years old used to go in the morning. At around 3pm we used to have a 20-minute break to have some snacks and play with our friends outside the classrooms. I used to love playing table tennis. It was very popular and I was quite good at it. But as much as I loved it, it was not my priority. As soon as the bell rang, I used to run to the school chapel on my own and spend at least 5 minutes talking to God in there. I learnt to make the sign of the cross as a good Catholic and I used to do that in front of the images. One day, a very old sister asked me not to do that as our worship should be to God alone. I never forgot that and I started changing my relationship with God. I stopped worshipping images and going to processions because I did not feel comfortable walking behind the images and singing anymore, but I carried on going to the morning service as usual.

When I was 14 years old, I heard God's voice again. I was in my last year before going to high school. God told me that he was going to take me across the ocean. I felt it very strongly in my heart and I kept it with me. This time I could not talk to my parents about it. I could not just ask my mum to take me. Can you imagine my dad's reaction if I had told him? I wasn't allowed to leave our house by myself. How would I be allowed to cross the ocean by myself at the age of 14? My world was very small at that time, I was very young, and I could not even imagine that once I became an adult, I was going to make my own decisions and it wasn't going to be my parents' decision anymore. I had no knowledge and maturity to know how God works; I didn't know God's time is different from our time. That He could take 2, 10 or even 21 years to take me abroad and that is what it took to happen, 21 years for God to take me across the ocean. 21 years was necessary to prepare me for what He had planned for me. This reality was far, far away from my small teenager world which used to consist of going to school, staying home and spending my Sunday afternoons at my grandmother's house. I used to love going there even though I could not play with my cousins on the street. I was happy spending time inside the house with my aunts, uncles and grandmother and helping my aunts to look after their little children and babies. Sometimes my cousins used to come for a bit before running off to go to play on the streets. I used to entertain myself in the garden writing maths equations on the wall pretending to be at school. Please do not misunderstand me, I was a happy girl.

After God told me that He was going to take me across the ocean, I developed a desire to know more about Europe. I sent letters to some countries' embassies asking for material about their countries. I received information from Poland and Spain and I treasured that material and read it. I knew one day I was going to leave my country, but I was not in a rush, I loved my family, and I was very close to my mum. I would put my life in line to protect her. She was a very vulnerable lady, loving and caring, very submissive. My parents thought I was just finding something else to learn about as I used to read a lot. The possibility of me leaving the country one day never crossed their minds.

In Luke 2:51

> *"...And his mother treasured up all these things in her heart."*

16

Just as Mary kept all her experiences with Jesus in her heart, I also did that.

I kept in my heart all the experiences I was having with God. I had a very special relationship with God, every night I used to kneel by my bed and pray before I went to sleep. I have always loved him, even not knowing him deeply, I always felt His presence in my life, and I have always been considerate to people, loving and caring. I have always enjoyed helping people when they are in need. I really like people a lot.

YOU ARE GOING TO HAVE CHILDREN BY ADOPTION

As I got older, I carried on living my life as normal as possible, but I kept an interest in Poland, Spain, and England.

When I was 18 years old, God spoke to me again and he told me that I was going to have children by adoption. Another piece of information that I kept in my heart. It used to puzzle me sometimes, because these thoughts were so far from my reality, my plans and my dreams. I had not even had a boyfriend yet; my dad wouldn't allow it. I had my first boyfriend when I was 20 years old and we were only together for six months. Then I had another one when I was 21 years old for another six months. I was very young and honestly, I did not want to get married too soon. I wanted to finish my education, I wanted to become a doctor and find a job, build up a career and then have a family. I did not understand at that point that it wasn't about my plans, but God was telling me about His plans for my life and they were a lot better than my plans.

Even though I started looking for God at an early age, at 6, I didn't understand that God can speak to all of us. God has a plan for each one of us, and His plans are far better than any of our plans. I loved

God, I used to speak to Him every day, but I still didn't have a strong relationship with Him. At that point I had no one to help me to understand His Word and, because I so badly wanted to be a doctor to help people, I had to study many hours daily, including Sundays, to achieve my goal. This area is highly competitive in Brazil and everybody who wants that career needs to study intensively.

> *John 6:45 (NIV) says "It is written in the Prophets: 'They will all be taught by God.' Everyone who has heard the Father and learnt from Him comes to me."*

I heard Him, I knew the messages were not from my mind, but I was not spending time to learn about Him, to get to know Him, to have an intimate relationship with my Father, it was not my priority. First, I needed to focus on getting to a medical school, and I set this as my primary goal of my life and I gave it everything I could. I knew one day I was going to get married, and I was expecting to get married to a widower or a divorced man with children, so I could help him to raise his children. But the two boyfriends I had were single young men around my age. It was a constant battle trying to fulfil my own dreams instead of trusting in God's plans for my life.

Today I am a mature woman and I know how important it is to learn from God to be able to grow into the image of Christ. I understand now that salvation is not about a place where I want to get, heaven; but it is about the person God wants me to become, a better version of myself, by having a renewed and transformed mind, an image of Christ, His Holy Son.

I GAVE MY LIFE TO JESUS

Job 42:5

> *"My ears had heard of you, but now my eyes have seen you."*

In July 1989, I gave my life to Jesus at the age of nearly 23 years old. It was a difficult time in my life, I was getting better after a mild breakdown due to excessive studying to try to get into medical school. I did not make it in, I will talk more about that later, but today I understand why I could not get into the medical school. That July I achieved third place in a Business Management entrance exam and I also realised that I really wanted to know more about God. At that time, the Catholic Church did not used to give deep bible studies and I was longing for that. A friend of mine invited me to go to an Evangelical church with her. I started going there and a few months later, because I was feeling empty, that I needed something more, I talked to a lady from the church, Ana Claudia. We became friends and I told her I wanted to have what she had, I wanted to have Jesus in my life and to know more about Him. From that moment on, my life started to take another direction after I took this turning point. It was a fantastic one!

Soon, I was very involved in the church and with the young people. I was very happy despite not enjoying my degree course, but I was determined to finish it, to go all the way with it. I wanted to teach myself about determination. One year later, my pastor asked me to leave the church. He felt that his church was not a good match for me as I was quite outgoing and my vision for social work at the church was so different to theirs. It was not easy for me; I remember how bad I felt. For two weeks I went for long walks to think about my life and to try to understand what I did wrong. I was feeling very unworthy. I did not understand at that time that this was part of God's plan. He allowed that to happen because I had to move to another church for His plan to be fulfilled in my life. Today I can see that, and I am in touch with that beloved pastor and his wife. God used them in my life to help me to make a move in the right direction, towards His purpose for my life.

I used to teach maths and physics to a young man who wanted to do the entrance exam to go to a military university. I was sad and told him what happened to me so he told me about his new church. It was a new church where he was confident that I was going to be welcome and to fit well. He told me to book an appointment with Pastor Paulo Borges Junior, from Sal da Terra Church. He was in his early thirties and he was the senior pastor. I went to the church office and I asked to talk to him. He was there and he spoke to me, no appointment needed. I told him what happened, I could not look in his eyes, I remember that I was feeling ashamed, and I asked him if his church would receive me and if I could go there. At first, he was finding it difficult to believe my story and he asked me if it was true. I had my diary with me, and I handed it to him showing my former pastor's phone number and I said: "This is his phone number, you can ring him and talk to him. I am sure he is going to confirm my story." So, he said it was not necessary and that of course I could go to his church. He suggested I start attending his church one week from the following Sunday as they were moving to a much closer venue to where I lived.

I stayed at that church for 12 years, until the day I moved to England, where I became a missionary at Salt Church in Bolton which, incidentally, used to be part of Sal da Terra Church.

GOD TOLD ME AGAIN: I AM TAKING YOU ACROSS THE OCEAN

Genesis 12:1

> *The LORD had said to Abram, "Leave your country, your people and your father's household and go to the land I will show you."*

When I was around 27 years old God spoke to me again about taking me across the ocean. This time He was clear about the country; He showed me in a dream that He was going to bring me to the North of England and after that he was going to take me to the South West of England. I could see the map of England in my dream. In another dream he showed me an area in that city, Uberlandia, which goes all the way up to a hill. I moved to the top of the area and after that, I moved to South West of the area. This area is better and more desirable than where I used to live. We can see that the area represents England which has got a better quality of life than Brazil and the area I used to live.

God also used a prophecy to speak to me. My church in Brazil had a fasting and prayer campaign when every Home Group used to go to the top of a hill to pray after 10pm. The week our Home Group went to the top of this hill, we met another group from my church. In this other group there was a pastor who was my friend's stepfather. He and his wife had just moved back to Uberlandia and I had never met him before and did not know him at all. He came to me during the prayer time and said:

> *"God is telling me that He is going to separate you to work for Him in the church and after that He is going to take you across the ocean"*

21

I felt the anointing of God filling me up from top to bottom. I kept that in my heart with the other messages, but this time I shared it with a couple of close friends from the university, telling them that one day I was going to leave Brazil for good as a missionary. When I talk to my friends who do not have the same faith as me, I talk to them at the same level as if they did have the same faith. My friends Regiana and Marcelo remember what I told them. Regiana told me that when I met her again through social media a few years ago. She commented that it had really happened exactly as I had told them at the University.

YOU ARE GOING TO HAVE A CHILD OF YOUR OWN FLESH

After this experience at the hill, the first part of the prophecy came true. I started working for my church as part of the TV programme team. We used to have a 30-minute TV programme and I did lots of different things for them like the finances, programme production and the programme schedule. I used to love it.

We also used to be part of the team that organised a camping event for 800 people over the carnival holiday. Usually, Christians from Evangelical backgrounds don't go to the carnival, instead Evangelical churches organise their own events away from the cities and the carnival celebration. It is very popular over there and I was at one of these camping events, working with the team that organised the event. I was part of a team that used to prepare the camping TV programme which used to go on the screen before the service in the marquee. I was passing by this tent, during the morning service, and the leaders were praying for people. I could feel the anointing of God and Cristina and her husband, who were leaders of Sal da Terra, were ministering there during that time along with other leaders, were praying individually for each person at the event. I was feeling exhausted and sad. I was already 31 years old and by myself. All the single men in my church just wanted to be friends with me. I tried to get close to a couple of them and I heard that friendship was all they could offer me. I didn't used to go on dates. I went once and I was so desperate to find the right person that I nearly fell out in my purpose to keep myself for my husband only. He was not a boyfriend and he did not have an intention to have a relationship with me. I could not see that I was expecting to have a relationship, but he just wanted to take the opportunity to benefit himself and I nearly allowed him to have it, with no strings attached. I nearly allowed him to have something that was very important to me. I dreamed of having a honeymoon certain that my husband was the only man I fully enjoyed. God had mercy on me and brought me out of that situation. It was painful and shameful. It was hard, but it helped me to become stronger, as per Romans 8:28:

> *"And we know that all things work together for good to those who love God, to those who are called according to His purpose."*

I knew that, but it did not make the waiting time easier. I started praying for my husband at the age of twenty-four after my relationship with my last boyfriend ended. Well, 7 years had passed, and I was still waiting, praying, and longing for my family and my biological clock was nearly running its last lap in my race to become a mum. For me, to become a mum was not just a case of having a fun time with someone. It was necessary to meet the right person, to get to know this person, to get married, settle down and then have a child together. I wanted to take the old-fashioned path to have a family. I wanted God's way to have a family, as I know it is safer, more complete. It is good.

Let us go back to the meeting at the camp. When I was passing by the tent and felt God's anointing, I heard God's voice telling me to ask Cristina to pray for me. She was so anointed that she had her eyes closed all the time while praying for people one by one. So, I waited for my turn and I stepped forward close to her, in front of her. She did not open her eyes, but she felt someone different was there. She started praying for me and suddenly she said God is saying:

"I will give you a child of your own flesh and blood."

I started crying, I was very sad and my shoulders felt so heavy and burdened. I cried a lot; her words came over me and filled my spirit like the fresh and living water of a river. I felt relieved of that weight on my shoulders, I felt anointed, loved, and cared for by my Father in heaven and washed by my tears.

God is a loving and caring Father, He always comes at the right moment to embrace us, to show His love, to show His appreciation, to reassure us that we are not forgotten and to remind us that His timing is different to our timing.

CHAPTER 3

GOING THROUGH THE STORM

In Matthew 14:23-31, God's word says:

When Jesus dismissed the people, he went up alone to a mountain to pray. Later that night, he was there alone, and the boat was already a considerable distance from land, battered by the waves, because the wind was blowing against it.

Shortly before dawn, Jesus went out to them, walking on the water. When the disciples saw him walking on the sea, they were terrified. "It is a ghost!" they said and cried out and they screamed in fear.

But Jesus immediately said to them, "Courage! That is me. Don't be afraid!"

"Lord," Peter said, "if it is you, send me to meet you over the waters."

"Come," he answered.

Then Peter got off the boat, walked on the waters, and went towards Jesus. But when he noticed the wind, he was afraid, and began to sink, he cried, "Lord, save me!"

Immediately Jesus reached out and held him. And he said, "Man of little faith, why did you doubt it?"

The disciples were going through a storm in the sea, a frightening situation to be in. This is just one example of a storm we could go through. Let us consider other types of storms in our lives like depression, death, anxiety, financial pressure, relationship issues, problems with our children, the list goes on.

Honestly, whatever the storm, it is very hard to go through it and sometimes it can even bring a feeling of abandonment, loneliness. The strong wind of our individual storm can blind us and make us feel lost, with no sense of direction.

But the message I would like to leave for you, which I also remind myself, is that in any circumstances we find ourselves in; God is with us.

God does not abandon us; He is the provider of everything, and He has provided everything we need.

When we understand that, we go through the storm with a different attitude, feeling calm and safe. It does not make the process in our lives any easier, but, on the other hand, the certainty that God never abandons us will bring comfort to our hearts.

God is good, God is complete, and He has a purpose in everything He allows us to go through.

He wants us to grow as a person, to grow in maturity, to become a better version of ourselves and to be a perfect expression of God's virtue in other people's lives.

When Jesus walked towards the boat, the sea was rough. The word of God says that the boat was a considerable distance from the land, and it was buffeted by the waves because the wind was blowing against it. Jesus does not let himself feel unsettled by the circumstances around Him. Despite that strong storm, He went to meet the boat while walking on the water. The disciples were terrified when they saw Jesus walking on the water, so Peter asked Jesus to allow him to walk on the waters with Him. Peter wanted to make sure it was Jesus coming in their direction and not a ghost. Jesus said: "Come."

Peter, looking at Jesus, got to do the impossible. Peter went to meet with Jesus, walking on the waters. Could you imagine how amazing this experience could be? At the same time, it could be frightening if we are not prepared to do it in faith, if we are not focused on what Jesus is doing in our lives, if we don't keep our eyes firmly fixed on Jesus and if we do not totally, completely trust that He is with us and nothing is going to come out of His control. Remember what happened to Peter, he suddenly began to look at the circumstances around him, he looked at the strong storm, he felt the strong and cold wind against his skin, and he was hearing the loud voice of the winds and waves caused by that terrifying storm. When he took his eyes off Jesus and he began to sink and to drown.

When we are in the middle of a storm it is necessary to look at Jesus all the time and not to the circumstances around us. Even if it looks like there is no solution and no hope. We must fix our eyes on the author and consummate of our faith, Jesus.

In my walking with Jesus, I have learned that my happiness comes from him, regardless of my situation and the circumstances which I find myself in. My favourite place is always the centre of God's will, it is there where I have joy in the Lord and then when I am living my life with purpose. I need to remember that God never promised me that Christianity would be easy, and that I would not endure hardship in my Christian life sometimes. What God promised me is that He will never forsake me, and He will help me to safely go through every single storm I have in my journey.

I am sharing with you some of the storms I have had to go through because I believe that they were part of my journey, intended to mould me and to help me to become a better version of myself; in the same way that I believe the trials you may endure in life, as a Christian, will work to mould and grow you. Remember that all these storms occurred after I gave my life to Jesus and accepted Him as my Lord.

MY FAMILY FINANCES

After my sixth birthday, my parent's financial situation started improving and my dad was able to build a lovely house that we moved to. He stopped being a builder to become a project manager and a trader. That brought a time of prosperity to my family. I was privately educated and my dad was very generous with his children, but he wasn't very wise in how to invest his money. My eldest brother always asked him to invest in properties, to build a portfolio of flats and shops for rent and he could have done that, but he did not listen to my brother and instead, he lent money to

28

people in financial difficulty and used to receive interest monthly. It was a lot of money. At that time, in the 80s, the Brazilian economy was very unsettled. One presidential election when I was 20 years old was enough to make my dad lose around 50% of his money overnight. It was New Year's Day 1987, millions of people, including my dad, lost millions because of the new president's economy plan. Some of my dad's friends could not take the impact and took their own lives, there were around five friends. My dad had some bad attitudes that used to drive me mad, but there are some other attitudes I really admire in him. My dad is a strong man, he did not choose a quick escape by taking his own life. My dad faced the problem and accepted he could lose everything if it were necessary, but he would not cause any damage to his honest character. He would rather become poor and start everything again than stain his name. I really admire that; I have learned that from him. If someone is going to lose something, why not me?

Six years later and yet another economy plan from another president, and my dad lost the rest of his assets, keeping just a small farm which was not very good. It had a big impact on our family, and I learned to live with little and to budget wisely. I graduated in Business Management, it wasn't my plan to become an executive, but I was a very good employee, competent, honest and loyal. Despite that, I would not last more than a year in any job and I could not understand why this was happening to me. It is simple, God was preparing me to work for the church and later to bring me overseas. He was giving me the opportunity to have experience in different situations to learn life skills which were going to be useful tools in my life in the UK.

At one time when I was replacing a maths teacher in a secondary school; my eldest brother and I used to live together, and my parents and youngest brother were living with us. It was at the time when my dad had lost the rest of his money and ended up with debts. My dad, my mum and my youngest brother moved out to the farm because my dad could not face the fact that he did not have any money to pay his debt. That was too much for him, it was killing him inside. So, my brother and I decided to take responsibility for his debt because he was desperate, and we could not bear to see him like that.

Because of that we did not have much to eat at home. My brother used to eat at his office, (the company he worked for used to give free meals to staff) and I used to eat at the school. In Brazil, all schools offer free meals to students of all ages and staff. After we finished paying off his debt, 10 months later, I went to the farm and I asked them to come back home. God is good and we could start living again as a family.

Psalm 23:1:

> *"The LORD is my shepherd; I shall not be in want."*

Around about the time of my 26th birthday this verse did not make sense to me. My family was in a difficult financial situation and I was alone, I just could not find anyone who I could build my life with. I used to have lots of male friends and they just used to see me like that; a good friend who they could trust. I used to see them like that too, but outside my friendship circle there were a couple of young men in the church that got my attention, one at a time, but I was far from their ideal woman. Today I can see that one of them got married to the right person, and I have not heard about the other one, I lost contact with him, anyway, I was wrong about both of them.

Before my 24th birthday I did not want to get married, it was the last thing on my priority list. Suddenly, after my 24th birthday I started wanting to have my own family, but I was really scared to marry the wrong guy. At that point, I was more mature, and God had been speaking to me about his many amazing sons who were willing to have a family and who were family men. They were loving and caring and would be a good husband and father. He showed me a few men and I started to pray and fast for the right man for me, I didn't want to choose, I did not want to take the chance and get it wrong because I did not trust my judgement. I wanted Him to choose for me.

But one thing I did not consider when I prayed, is that when we put things in God's hands, we need to trust Him completely and rest because God's timing is different to my, your or anyone else's timing.

2 Peter 3:8:

> *"With the Lord a day is like a thousand years, and a thousand years are like a day."*

His time and His choice are a perfect match for each one of us, but we need to be prepared to wait. I had to wait, and I had to learn to wait. It caused me a lot of sorrow, because I wanted to be a mum and I was heading into my thirties which meant that my biological clock was slowing down. This is normal in a woman's life, but God expects us to totally trust him. He knows what He is doing, and He is never late.

In John 11:4 when Jesus heard that Lazarus, His friend, was sick he said:

> *"This sickness will not end in death. No, it is for God's glory so that God's Son may be glorified through it."*

When Jesus arrived in Bethany, Lazarus was dead, and he had been in the tomb for four days. Martha went to meet Jesus and she said in verse 21 *"Lord if you had been here, my brother would not have died. But I know that even now, God will give you whatever you ask."*

Jesus said in verse 23: *"your brother will rise again."* And He did.

Martha's first comment makes us believe that she was blaming Jesus for that situation. If He had come earlier, as soon as He heard His friend needed Him, His friend would not be dead. But Jesus wasn't late, He was at the right place, at the right time, so that the son of God could be glorified. God's glory would be manifested and people would believe that Jesus is in fact His son.

Timing can bring a lot of anxiety and sorrow to our soul when we don't totally trust God, when we do not understand that His plans for our lives do not involve just us individually or those immediately around us. God has got a bigger picture, and it involves His church everywhere. So, all the plans God had already revealed to me at that point, were not just for me. He uses my life to benefit other people's lives and He uses different people's lives to benefit my life, so that I can benefit other lives and so on. It keeps going and at the end, all His family around the world will be impacted for His glory.

His purpose is for the whole of humankind, and we are part of that plan. Our purpose will get together with other people's purposes to become one big, whole, complete, fulfilled purpose.

Another thing we need to consider is that because God chooses the right person for us to share our lives with and direct us in our purpose, it doesn't mean it is an easy option to deal with, but it is guaranteed that it will last, because God is faithful and He will give us a perfect match, not a perfect person. He knows us deeply; He knows our hearts and what we need and not just what we want. I truly advise any person to wait for God's choice but, be ready to wait if it is necessary. He can give you this wish in one week, month, year or in 13 years, as in my case. Jacob waited for 14 years for his first choice and Abraham waited 25 years for his breakthrough. He was 75 years old when he left Haran to go to the Promised Land. By the time Isaac was born, he was 100 years old. My waiting time was 13 years of fasting, prayers and crying for my husband.

Sometimes, I used to think that maybe God had forgotten me, that maybe it was not going to happen for me. But I did not lose heart, I persevered, and I used to be happy for my friends and I even helped some of them to organise their weddings. That attitude used to bring joy into my heart, honestly.

During one young adult's meeting at church, I confess I cried a lot. Lazaro and Flavia are an amazing couple, and they were a blessing to me that night. I told them about my family's financial situation and my desire to meet someone I could share my life with, I was feeling very unhappy. I really wanted to settle down, to have my own family and to see my parents in a better financial situation. Lazaro calmly opened his bible and read Psalm 23:1:

"The LORD is my shepherd; I shall not be in want."

He asked me, "Do you understand that?"

I said "No, I do not understand that."

"You have Jesus in your life, and He must be enough for you, you need to rest and let Him do the work for you. He will provide what your family needs and He will give you the right person who you will share your life with. Put your trust in Him and rest, let God's peace come into your heart."

That was not what I was expecting to hear. Maybe I wanted a magical formula. I went back home feeling bad and I wasted my precious young adult life feeling sorry for myself, being unhappy and miserable, but I would not leave God's presence. I could not bear to live my life outside of His presence, I was one hundred per cent sure about that. I would rather be alone than walk away from Him. That was for sure!

MY MUM'S HEALTH STARTED TO DETERIORATE

My mum's health started getting bad after my mid-20s. She was diagnosed with osteoporosis, diabetes, a heart problem, blood pressure and cancer. When the doctor, my dear friend Gisela, told me my mum had cancer. I felt as if my boat was sinking. I was very close to my mum; she was my best friend, my main inspiration, my companion. We used to spend about an hour talking every night before I went to bed. We used to talk openly about everything. I could not bear the idea of losing her. After I left the consultation room, I went to my doctor's waiting room for my consultation. I sat there waiting for my appointment with my eyes closed and praying. During that storm I heard God's voice telling me loudly and clearly that He was going to heal my mum and He did. She had surgery done, with no need for radio- or chemotherapy. It was amazing!

The bible says in Philippians 4:6-7:

> *"Do not be anxious about anything, but in every situation, by prayer and petition, with thanksgiving, present your requests to God.*
>
> *And the peace of God, which transcends all understanding, will guard your hearts and your minds in Christ Jesus."*

I also experienced the love of God through my close friends and my church. We did not have money to pay for my mum's surgery and we did not want to wait for the Public Health System, as the list was one year long. My mum had stage 5 cancer already, so we needed to be proactive. My friends helped me to organise a fundraiser lunch on a Sunday after the morning service and lots of people came to support us and some gave offerings. We did not have money to buy the material to cook the food for this lunch, some friends donated what we needed and a couple of other friends cooked the meal and I helped in everything I could. In one meal we were able to raise the money we needed, and she had her surgery done by the best specialist in town at that time.

> *Ephesians 3:20: "Now to him who is able to do immeasurably more than all we ask or imagine, according to his power that is at work within us."*

Psalm 37:4

One day I was crying in church because of the situation I mention above, and my pastor's wife Cristina gave me a piece of paper. When I opened that piece of paper, I was sobbing, and I read it.

It was Psalm 37:3-4:

> *"Trust in the Lord and do good; dwell in the land and enjoy safe pasture. Take delight in the Lord, and he will give you the desires of your heart."*

God bless you Cris, you are a blessing in my life, but, honestly, at first, I did not understand what was written on that paper. The reason is because I thought I was already living like that. I thought I was already doing good and enjoying God's presence, so I could not understand that.

My heart was in the wrong place and I did not see that. I thought about that verse in the wrong way, I was trying to please God to benefit myself. This was not only wrong, it was sad and very selfish. I cannot try to trade with God, I cannot say to God I have been a "good girl", so now, please, give me what I want, wish, and desire. It does not matter how caring and sweet I sounded. It does not work like that. God is not Father Christmas waiting for my wish list to know exactly what to give me for Christmas. This a childish way to think and to live. It shows how shallow my relationship with God was. This was not about me, my needs and desires.

It should be, in fact, about me having a deep and mature relationship with God to the point that my will would be in perfect and natural line with His will.

The reason for that is because I would become one with Christ as Christ is one with His Father. In other words, I would become an image of Christ and be able to express and transmit God's virtues where I go and through whatever I do as Christ Jesus did.

After finding our purpose in life we can grow as a person and live a fulfilled life. But how do I know what it is right for me? In the next chapter I will talk about the different plans in my life and how God's plan prevailed above all others.

CHAPTER 4

WHICH PLAN WOULD
SUIT ME BETTER?

"For I know the plans I have for you," declares the Lord, "plans to prosper you and not to harm you, plans to give you hope and a future." (Jeremiah 29:11)

MY DAD'S PLAN

My dad's dream was to have a child trained to be a doctor, engineer, lawyer, or dentist. None of the other professions were good enough in his mind. So, he really invested in our education, he worked hard and provided for a private education for all his five children. But, in the end it was just my eldest brother and I who went to university and we did not study any of his choices. My brother became an accountant and I studied Business Management. We both tried to please our dad, we studied hard to get into medical school.

In Brazil, one must go through an entrance exam to go to university and I failed it 13 times in different cities. Once, I did the test for two different universities in the same day for three days; I spent the whole morning and afternoon doing the test. I was exhausted after three days and I failed both, of course. It was a crazy idea. I was not very good at managing these big exams. My mind used to go blank. One time I could not read the test, so I put random answers on the answer sheet and left the room. After I had gone, I read and answered all the questions. In four years of trying to get into medical school I managed to help four friends to do exactly that, by teaching them some of the subjects they could not understand, but I personally could not get into it! I used to feel sad about my results, but at the same time very happy for my friends. I remember going to school once to get a result and as usual I failed but my friend. who was one of the friends I helped, had passed and she did not know yet. I nearly ran all the way to her house to tell her the news. When I got there, she was still in bed so I woke her up and I was so happy for her and she was over the moon. We ran back to the school to celebrate and we danced to carnival music there together with all the other young people. I could not celebrate my result, but I could not miss the opportunity to celebrate my friend's success. I was genuinely happy for her. She could not understand that, why I was there with her and not in my home sad. I left her at the party after a while when people started to get drunk, I was not comfortable with that. She stayed there, and I did what I always used to do after failing these exams. I went for a walk and then, to the cinema by myself and I watched a film, this was how I used to cry about my failure. It used to make me feel better, to take my mind off of my sadness and to go on a journey through the fantasy world of the big screen.

After four years of trying to pass this big test, I had a mild breakdown, my teacher could not understand how I used to fail, because I was such a good, dedicated, and bright student, but I know now that it wasn't God's plan for me. It was my dad's plan and it failed. After my breakdown, I did the test to get onto the Business Management course and I had the second-best score. I did not like the course, but I now understand why I had to study that. God was preparing me for what I was going to face ahead in my life and honestly, although I am good at office work, I never intended to become an executive. My qualification has been much needed since God separated me to work for the church in Brazil and in Bolton UK, where I also used to work for the church. Nowadays, I also run my own small business as a childminder and what I learnt has been very useful to me. We do not have to understand everything but trust that God has the best for us, and His vision is wider than ours. We just see our environment around us, yet He sees beyond the whole universe.

MY PLAN

Despite all the conflict inside myself and the problems with my family's finances and my mum's health, I used to work a lot for the church in different areas like helping to organise camps during the carnival season and others camps in general, performing drama in churches and in theatres, schools, and outside spaces. They were all outreaches, to take the good news about the gospel everywhere we were invited. I also used to be involved in helping the social work team to organise fundraising events for our charity work over there. I was a faithful servant at the church and another part of God's revelation was confirmed. I was separated by God to work full time for the church and sooner or later, God was going to take me across the ocean. It was just a matter of time. I was responsible for overseeing four of the five crèches they used to have, including doing their monthly budget and I was also used for other finance duties in the office. The church used to have around 250 children from a poor background in the four crèches I used to oversee. I also used to write new projects and take them to the council office to get their support in expanding the social work. I was very busy, but I never complained, I used to work hard and I really enjoyed my job. Salt of the Earth church is going to be forever in my heart. I love it.

So, in my mind I had a perfect and strong reason to stay there, it was beautiful and rewarding work. And in my mind at that time it would have been even more perfect to meet the right man, who loves God as much as I did and to have had three or four children. We would have lived in the same city as my parents, and this would mean that we could visit them every Sunday like we used to do with my grandmother when I was a child growing up until I moved to Uberlandia. I wanted to carry on that tradition and teach my children to love and respect their grandparents. I also wanted to be there to look after my mum in case she needed me. She was already very vulnerable, different from my dad who was a very strong and healthy man.

But if my plans had come true, my family wouldn't be my amazing family and I wouldn't change them for anything, they are my world.

GOD'S PLAN VS MY PLAN

The strong bond I had with my church and all my commitment and loyalty with the work of God made it very hard to understand Psalm 37:4:

> *"Trust in the Lord and do good; dwell in the land and enjoy safe pasture. Take delight in the Lord, and he will give you the desires of your heart."*

Despite all the enjoyment with my work, I used to feel something was missing and I was unhappy. I could not understand why I was still alone in my early thirties. In my mind I was already being good, I was working so hard trying to please God, on top of that I had been praying for over six years and He still had not given me the desire of my heart. Why I was alone? Why was I so unhappy and still without my own family?

All the things I mentioned in chapter three used to make me feel very unhappy. I used to come to church and sit by myself. I assumed no one wanted to sit next to me, nobody liked me, and there was nothing special in my life to attract people's attention. My self-esteem was low and it made me spend too much time feeling sorry for myself. Have any of you had this feeling? It is awful! I also used to think that if there is someone in here who likes me, this person should make a move and sit down next to me. Today, when I look back, I ask myself, why was it that way? Why couldn't I make a move? I never took the time to think about the other person at that time. Maybe, the other person was also feeling like I was and waiting for me to make a move and show some kindness. Why couldn't I be the person to make a move? I wasted so many years during my twenties feeling sorry for myself instead of trying to make a difference, helping, and embracing people in their suffering and confusion.

You may think that I was good at relationships because I worked in social work, but it is not like that. Although someone can help other people, it does not mean that this person is good at developing relationships and being sensitive to other people's needs. I was very good at helping people, I loved it, but when it came to developing relationships, I wasn't good. I was always trying hard to be accepted, to please people, to have a feeling of belonging. I had low self-esteem.

Because I was sad and miserable, I was spending too much time thinking about myself, assuming some things that were not true and looking at the circumstances around me, instead of keeping my eyes on Jesus, the pioneer and perfecter of my faith. We need to look at Jesus to find pleasure in being in God's presence, to trust Him, to spend less time thinking about ourselves and to try to think about others and what we can do to help and to make a difference in people's lives. An attitude like that makes all the difference in our lives. It makes us feel good about ourselves and we become a better person. We also then source our esteem in Him.

At that time, I could not understand that God works in a different way to us. His plans do not just involve my life, but He has got a much wider picture of His plans. His vision goes beyond my understanding and I do not have to understand everything. I must know Him deeply and by knowing Him I can trust Him completely and I can know that everything He allows in my life is for my own good and for the benefit of a wider group of people around me. This goes on until it reaches all the people in the earth. He was preparing me for something bigger and I needed to stop doing so much for so many people and listen to Him and develop a deeper relationship with Him. I was overdoing it and I was not taking time to listen to my Father, to understand what He wanted for me. I was too worried and too busy with the work of God and I forgot to spend time with the God of the work. My pain was the result of my lack of intimacy with God.

I was tired of living through other people's experience. I wanted to have my own experience, then, one day, I prayed and said to God,

"God I do not want to live my life just through other people's stories by listening to their amazing testimonies of how their lives have changed." I wanted to have my own testimony and to be able to tell others my story about what God has been doing in my life. But I did not want to obey God, I wanted His will to line up to my will under my conditions, my rules, my expectations, my…my…my…my…me, me, me, me. Everything in my mind was about me. I was ignoring God, I was not listening to Him, I was overdoing, overactive but I was not being proactive, doing what I had to do, what He told me to do.

Do you remember that God brought some revelations into my life? Most of them had come true in my mid-thirties and I honestly was not longing to come over to the UK. On the other hand, I really wanted to have my own family, but there in Brazil. I kept in my heart the part about crossing the ocean and I never told my parents; in fact, I just told a couple of friends. Before I came to England, I used to talk to God about that: "Lord, what am I going to do there? I like helping people, doing social work here, where my family and I live. There are so many people in need here; and over there, people don't need someone like me, I have nothing to offer them. They have everything they want and need. Don't you think, God, that maybe it will be better if I stay here and carry on doing what I am doing? At the end of the day, I am responsible for four crèches here and all of them are in poor areas with around 250 children being looked after by us. And there are so many more plans and dreams waiting to be achieved. I will be more useful here and I absolutely love my job. And on top of staying and carrying on doing what I loved I could be close to my parents and help them." All of them were very good reasons, but for God it did not make any difference, because He could easily replace me for someone else that would do an even better job than me and that is what He did. Church social work over there a is very big deal, and as all projects had to have papers submitted to the authorities for approval and fund raising, I had somehow believed that I was the only one who could do this work. In fact, I eventually realised that I needed to accept that my time there had finished and that it wasn't part of His plan for my life anymore. He had other plans to fulfil in my life.

God wants more from me; He wants me to get to know Him deeply and trust Him even when I don't understand His plans. I just need to know that He will always have the best for me.

God is God and if He wanted, He could have given me my own family there, nearby my Brazilian family.

Yes, He could have if He wanted to, but He did not want that for me, and I am so happy for that because I wouldn't have the lovely family I have now. I am pleased He didn't give me what I wanted, because what He wanted is always the best. Today I can see the bigger picture. There is no shadow of a doubt that I was trying to negotiate with God, trying to convince Him of which place would be the best for me. I am so glad God did not accept my suggestions, otherwise my family would not have been the family I have right now, and I would never change that now. My husband would not be my lovely husband, Martin; Joao-Lucas, our lovely and kind son wouldn't exist, and our gorgeous girls would exist, but they wouldn't be with a family that love them as much as we do, because we are the best match for them. They are part of the new season God has for me; they are part of God's plan in my life; and they would be living a different life if I had rebelled against God's will.

It is God's plan for the five of us to be the family we are today, and He always has the best for each one of us.

Can you see the big picture in your life? I could only see my life around me at the time when I was living in Brazil, but God could see the life ahead of me. He could see my husband and the good match we are for each other and, He could see Joao-Lucas's birth, He has prepared plans and a life for our beloved son. God could also see Mia and Maisie's birth and how much they would need Martin and I to look after them, to give them a better life, a better opportunity. God's plans did not involve only my life, He could not have given me that in Brazil.

I had to come, I had to leave everything behind, I had to trust in God and to rest in His hands and let Him do the rest.

I needed to accept that staying in Brazil was not God's plan for my life, and I did not need to understand everything I just had to trust Him. I used to have a servant mind, trying to do what I thought was the best for my life, for myself, for my parents.

God wanted more from me, God wanted me to understand that I am His daughter and not His servant. A servant tries only to do what He is expected to do in his job, he does not have an intimate relationship with the Master. Their relationship is based on productivity, loyalty, respect, and reward. God expects more from me. As His daughter I need to do the best for my Father's business, or in other words, for my Father's salvation plan for humankind.

I have a part to play in His plan, Jesus came and did His part through his sacrifice on the cross. Now it is my turn to be Christ in people's lives, to be the expression of God's love by shining, translating, and showing God's virtues through my life, actions, and attitudes.

In another words, I need to be a live expression of God's love and His virtues in people's lives. As children, s, we need to go where the Father wants us to go because He knows best, and He knows us deeply and knows the desires of our heart. We need to stop everything we are doing for a moment to listen to Him, be ready to obey and to take action.

CHAPTER 5

MY PLAN SINKS

"Trust in the Lord and do good; dwell in the land and enjoy safe pasture. Take delight in the Lord, and he will give you the desires of your heart." Psalm 37:4

Sometimes we blame God for hardship, but we need to accept that there is purpose even in hardship and what we desire is going to be there for us if we will only walk in Him. It was necessary to accept change and to learn to believe that He will always be with me, even in the middle of the challenges of life. It is all part of His big plan, and all I needed to do was to accept that I am His daughter and as a daughter, everything that matters to my Father matters to me too. It is important to enjoy myself while I am helping my Father in his salvation plan for humankind and not do what I think He wants me to do, even if it is good. Unfortunately, I chose to do things my way, some things were very good and others were unwise.

ENGAGEMENT

My attitude brought the wrong man into my life who became my fiancé. I was about to get married to the wrong person to try to fulfil my plans, to live my life my way because God was taking too long and I was finding the waiting process too hard. In my mind I knew what the best for me was, I wanted to show God that I could live my life and make my own decisions and He as my Father would have to be there for me, to bless me, to turn my decisions into blessings. How arrogant I was! I was about to do whatever it took to stay there, even if it were to marry the wrong man and have children with him. I wanted that more than anything else along with being able to look after my parents and carry on working as a missionary in Uberlandia city, doing the wonderful work I used to love a lot.

I was blinded by my own desire to build a family and I could not clearly see the situation in front of me. That man was not what God had prepared for me and I was not happy in that relationship, I was trying hard to make it work and it was impossible for that to happen. Today, I can see that, and I know now through my own experience, how difficult it is to see God's plans when we are going through a process, because we want to convince God about our plans, and it is not easy to humble ourselves, stop, and listen to what He has to say.

This is one of the reasons you are reading my story today; so that I can tell you that God does not expect us to understand everything, but He expects us to have a close relationship with Him, to grow in knowledge about Him and His virtues and to get to know Him deeply enough to trust Him and to believe that He always wants the best for each one of us.

God has a purpose in all circumstances around us, He allows them to happen to shape us, to help us to see better, to grow in His knowledge and hopefully to achieve what we need to achieve in our lifetime.

In August 2001, I was finding it hard to carry on with my engagement. Our wedding was booked for 10th November 2001, I was going to be 35 in September 2001. In my small world it could be my last chance to have a family and I could not miss that opportunity. On the other hand, the unhappiness inside me was killing me. I felt in my heart that he was not the man for me, but the uncertainty of meeting someone in my mid-thirties, getting married and having children before my biological clock stopped ticking was driving me into that possible marriage disaster.

One night at the end of August, I was at home with my parents and for the first time I asked their opinion about my wedding. I had never asked them that question before and my dad said something that hit me more than if he had said I do not want and I do not approve of your wedding. I knew they did not approve of my engagement; this is the reason I never asked for their opinion. But that night I decided to ask and to listen to them for the first time about my fiancé. I wanted to hear from my biological father and my heavenly Father. So, my dad said in love: "This is not what we have dreamed for you, my daughter, but we will be with you, we will support you whatever you decide to do." I knew my biological dad and that reply did not seem to match what I knew of him. It was his voice combined with God's direction because God knows me better than anyone in my life. That answer really hit me hard and made me think about my decision and the consequences that it could bring into my life. I left the living room, and I went straight to my bedroom. I knelt on the floor, sobbing and praying. I was feeling lost, hopeless and I could not take it anymore. At that moment, God was not easy on me, but He was not mean either. He was firm and sharp with a disobedient daughter who thinks she knows better. Then, God challenged me, I clearly heard His voice "Do you want me to give you the desire of you heart?" I said "Yes please, I really want to have a family. I have been praying for 10 years and I am about to realise my dream, but I am not happy. Why is this happening? I work so hard for you, to please you. And I cannot feel joy inside of me." So, God told me to read Isaiah 1:19:

> *"If you are willing and obedient, you will eat the good things of the land."*

God carried on telling me: "You work hard for my kingdom doing things that I don't want you to do anymore. Your time here has finished, I have tasks for you to complete for your life elsewhere."

MY MUCH-LOVED JOB

The work I was doing in Brazil was amazing, it filled me with love and I knew that it was part of God's plan to prepare me, to mould me into the person He wanted me to become. But what I could not accept that this was not for life. Our life has got seasons and my season doing that job had finished and I did not want to let it go. Despite being a good and faithful servant, I was not irreplaceable. He would put the right person to do the work I was doing after I had left this position, and He did, God brought more than one person to do my work, because I could not see I was overdoing it. But God sees all things, His vision is wide and covers not just my life, but He sees everything. I brought on myself the hard time I was going through because of my disobedience to God. I wanted to carry on doing things in my own strength and wisdom, even after my time had finished in Brazil.

I was in a good and safe place, doing a fruitful work, but I was not being fully fruitful myself. It does not matter how good the place and the work are, if it is not at the centre of God's will for your life, you do not produce the best fruits God has for you.

MY BRAZILIAN FAMILY

My family was the hardest part to let go of. In my mind, no one could look after my mum better than I could. I used to stay with her, by her side, when she needed to stay overnight in hospital for treatments. I used to look after her medication and accompany her to doctor's visits. I used to help her to look after the house and to buy extra fruit and vegetables to make sure she would have enough good food to look after herself. I used to spend time talking to her every single night before going to bed. I loved my family and to leave my lovely mum to come to England was a huge challenge for me personally.

But I knew what God wanted from me; He had been telling me since I was 14 years old that when the time comes, He was going to take me across the ocean. The time had come, I needed to trust Him, to surrender to His will. I ended my engagement the day after the talk with my father; it was not easy breaking up, but God held me in His hands and with the help of my beloved and late pastor at that time, I did it. It was the end of August 2001. After that I trained someone else to replace me doing part of my job and my late pastor was doing the rest of my job. Having let go of my beloved job and family, I landed at Heathrow Airport on 28 November 2001, 18 days after the date I was supposed to have got married. I was alone, heartbroken and 25 kilograms heavier in a foreign land. I left a hot country and landed in England in autumn; it was a very cold one and it was my first trip abroad. It was a big step of faith into the unknown, I was totally trusting God, completely dependent on Him; just the way He wanted me to be. A new chapter of my life started here, and I would know soon if God's plan would bring me the contentment I had been longing for. I had to wait for a while to know the answer to this though.

The best of life

PART II

UNDERSTANDING
MY PURPOSE

My life in the UK

The best of life

CHAPTER 6

BEING PROACTIVE

"In the same way, was not even Rahab the prostitute considered righteous for what she did when she gave lodging to the spies and sent them off in a different direction?" James 2:25

I would like to use this scripture to share with you about a book I am reading "A 10-Week Journey to Becoming a Vessel God Can Use", by Donna Partow. It is amazing what I have learnt from her and it is encouraging me to write my journey too. I will try to summarise a bit of what I have learnt so far. God can use us regardless of our history, Rahab is one strong example of that. Rahab, the prostitute, married Salmon, a good man, and they had a son called Boaz, a righteous man. In Mathew 1 we can see that she is part of Jesus's genealogy, she is in the list of Jesus's grandmothers. Also, in Hebrew 11:31 (NIV): "By faith the prostitute Rahab, because she welcomed the spies, was not killed with those who were disobedient." She is on the wall of faith in between the giants like Abraham, Jacob, Moses, and David. Her story reveals to us that God can use the most unlikely person to fulfil His plans. Through her life God brought deliverance to the spies. Rahab's example tells us that our past mistakes do not matter, if we repent, obey, and listen to God. Anyone can be used by God and be part of His plan for humankind. Do not let your mistakes stop you from reaching your purpose and having a fulfilled life.

When we depend on God alone and not on ourselves, there are no limits for what God can do in our lives and through our lives.

When I ended my engagement, God told me that it was just the beginning of a new life for me and not the end of my dream. I had to do what Abraham did, get my belongings and cross the ocean as God has been telling me to do since I was 14 years old. Abraham had lots of things and people to take with him, I just took one piece of luggage weighing 22kgs and a handbag. Not a lot, really.

God was telling me to stop trying things for myself and just trust him 100% and obey him and He was going to give me the desires of my heart. He was going to give me the good things of the land He would take me to. He is good, and His love endures forever and that is the only thing that should matter to me.

When I landed at Heathrow airport on 28th November 2001, I was 35 years old, single and in a foreign country where I could not speak the language properly. Honestly, my English was very poor, very basic. Despite moving to the Queen's land, this is not a fairy-tale story. Just because God told me to do it, it does not mean I was not going to have problems. God never promised me a life without problems, He promised me a life with security and with the companion of the Holy Spirit. I heard Pastor Paulo Borges Junior, my dear Brazilian pastor saying that the Holy Spirit is like a helmet which builders wear. It does not stop a brick from being dropped on a builder's head, but it will give him the confidence that it will keep him safe and not let substantial damage happen to him when a brick falls on him.

God looks after us, He supports us, He help us to overcome difficult times, He will never abandon us, and He does not take us away from the process we need to go through to become the person He wants us to turn in to.

I left my city with just a small amount of cash and my airplane ticket. I decided to totally trust God. To my surprise, the church organised a farewell surprise dinner for me the night before I left. One hundred people came to the dinner party and people started giving me money for my journey. It was a lot of money in Brazil but because of the currency, it was enough money to live for one month in the UK. Having left Brazil on a sweltering 35-degree day, it was quite a shock to arrive to a freezing zero-degree day in London, and as it was 4 o'clock in the afternoon, it was already dark. It rained all the time, I had never experienced bad weather like that before. I had no job, not enough money. I could only buy £5 of food to last the whole week. Not buying food because you don't want it is different to not buying food because you don't have the money. I did some cleaning to replace a friend during her maternity leave but it wasn't enough to cover rent, English Language School, food and utility bills. So, I was tempted to walk away from God's plans again and try to make my own choice when I was offered a good job in London to work in a celebrity's house looking after and driving his four children and his wife. It was good money for me, nearly ten times more than I was making, and as I was going to live in their house, it meant it was rent free for me. The problem was that I couldn't go to school for the 15 hours required for English Language Student to be legal in the UK. God was teaching me obedience, perseverance, to stop doing things in my own strength and to trust Him.

It was a tempting offer, but I didn't have peace because of my visa situation, so I decided to ask God first and I asked a friend to pray with me. I was asking God to talk to me and tell me if He wanted to take me to London as I was living in Bolton at that time. I head God say clearly to me: "I have brought you here to walk with your head held up and with no fear. It is not my plan for you to hide and be illegal in a foreign land." I understood the message, picked up the phone and rang my friend who contacted me regarding the job and said, "Thanks for thinking of me, but I am not interested in the job." And suddenly God's peace came into my heart, even knowing that I didn't have enough money to buy food. I knew God would provide as He had been doing since the day I had made the decision to come to the UK. One week later I found a job at the Bolton Hospital Laundry. It didn't pay as much as the other job, but it was enough to cover my expenses, it allowed me to attend school and by 10pm I was back home to sleep. I didn't have to work after 10pm like other students, and I could go to school every day on a weekday and go to church on Sunday mornings, and it was walking distance from my home. I used to share a house with other Brazilian students who were all younger than me. One 21-year-old man was living with us and he told me, out of the blue, "Silesia you are going to get married to an English guy" and I said immediately, "Shut up, please. I don't want that. I want to marry a Brazilian guy, go back to Brazil, and live near my parents." From my reaction you can see that I was still a work in progress, I was growing step by step. I was finding it very hard to adapt to the UK because of the weather and I missed my family too. I was still questioning why God had brought me to this country, why I couldn't stay in my homeland and have a family there. I could be married there, but I was here, away from my family. I had dear friends who were a blessing to me, but I was homesick. So I asked God: "What's next?" God said, "I want you to learn to love this country and these people," and I genuinely did it.

With spring came the most beautiful flowers in gardens. On my walk to school and to the laundry I could not get enough of looking at the big variety of gardens and colourful hanging baskets outside some homes and businesses. The diversity of the bright colours and shapes started to move my heart and shake my emotions. There were more people on the street, they looked happier and more relaxed with no need to rush to avoid the rain and cold weather. When the sun was out people sat everywhere to eat their lunch outside and to make the most of the sun. I could not get enough of watching this scene and it was warming up my heart and making me smile regularly. I started to fall in love with the country, the people, and the culture. The kindness and respect English people have shown to me and to people around me is amazing. I started praying for this nation and asking God to use me here, to make a difference through my life even if it was just in one person's life. I wanted to be used by God and to be a blessing in this country. I started to organise Christian outreaches in Bolton. I trained a group of young people to do mime and I invited a friend from a church in Hereford with their dance group to come over and help us to do outreach on the street.

With the spring came a new opportunity for me and my job changed too. I was invited to work for the church part time, so I left my job at the laundry to work for the church as well as for the English Language School. I was their office assistant. I was so happy. I was comparing my life to a big puzzle which used to be all messed up and finally I started to see the pieces coming together nicely, smoothly, with no pressure. I didn't have a lot of money, but I had enough to live and I could send a small amount, monthly, back to help my family in Brazil, to make sure they would have at least the basics. People used to tell me that I was blossoming, my smile was beautiful. I was spending more time in God's presence, listening to Him, doing what He wanted me to do and being where He wanted me to be. People used to make comments about my smile because I was smiling a lot. One day I really asked, "God have you brought me here just to smile, what else can I do?" I wanted to do more, like I used to do in Brazil.

But God wanted to teach me something simple first, which I used to find hard to understand.

I am important and I am going to make a difference in people's lives for who I am and not just for what I do.

When we put our lives in the centre of God's will, there is joy and peace. Everything else starts falling into place like a big and perfect puzzle. Our relationship with Him grows and we enjoy spending time with him more and more.

I have learnt to really love God, to trust Him and to depend on Him. At the end of the day, I changed everything to be obedient to Him. I left my family, job, culture and ended my engagement to come to a foreign country, with a different culture, language, weather and with no family and job. I had some nice friends who helped me a lot along the way, but they had their lives too and did what they could to help me. One year after my arrival in England I went to visit my parents in Brazil to use my return ticket. My mum said something very impactful to me: "My daughter, God knows how much I suffered when you left, but I'd rather suffer and see you as happy as I am seeing you now than have you back and see you as unhappy as I used to see you." I will never forget her words and how much that touched me.

God's plan is perfect and the change, the feeling of achievement, the fullness and joy it brings to our lives is amazing and irreplaceable.

At this point I understood what had happened to Paul, he used to have a thorn in his flesh and it was painful. He asked God three times to bring deliverance to him, God heard him and said in 2 Corinthians12:9

> *"My grace is sufficient for you, for my power is made perfect in weakness."*

God's purpose doesn't rely on human strength, it is the other way around; the weaker the person, the bigger God's power is revealed, manifested. The reason for that is because God's grace is revealed through His love and all the glory will go to Him alone and it isn't frustrated by human mistakes. It also doesn't depend on people's ability.

God wanted me to become one hundred percent dependent on Him, and this is what happened. I had no job, no family and no husband to rely on, my language skills were poor and I couldn't communicate fluently. I found myself in a place with a very different culture and poor weather. I had to learn to adapt and to cope in this scenario, and do you know what? I started to feel joy, fulfilled, complete in this land which God had promised to bring me to 21 years ago.

God is good and His love endures forever.

CHAPTER 7

GOD IS GOOD, AND
HIS LOVE ENDURES FOREVER

In January 2003, I was back in the UK after spending 5 weeks with my family and friends, by this time I was 36 years old and still single. Once more, I left my family, friends, country and culture behind, but this time was different. I was genuinely happy, I was blossoming. God was fulfilling His purpose in my life and filling me up with joy and the Holy Spirit was directing me, guiding me and bringing me peace. I was undoubtedly heading to where God wanted me to be and doing what He wanted me to do. I was in the centre of God's will and I finally understood Psalm 37:4

> *"Take delight in the Lord, and He will give you the desires of your heart."*

I was older than before, still single, but I was happy, I was enjoying God's presence. I realised that my joy does not depend on people and in the circumstances around me. My joy comes from God.

I used to go to Salt Church in Bolton where Marcos Barros and his wife, Neneta, were the pastors, when a Mexican couple visited the church and the wife was a prophet. She was preaching and giving messages to some people, when she suddenly asked who the church secretary was. People pointed to me and I lifted my hand up. She turned to me and said:

> "My faithful servant, by the end of the year you are going to have the desire of your heart."

Wow...I wasn't expecting that. I kept that word in my heart and carried on doing what God wanted me to do. In March 2003 I put my profile on a Christian dating website, and as I prayed first, I was at peace, the waiting process wasn't as painful as it used to be. I did not have money to pay for the dating website, but I managed to get 20 days free of charge. I said: "God if you have someone for me through this website, please show me during these 20 days as I am not going to carry on after that. I cannot afford it." I only had enough income to cover my expenses, I couldn't add extra expenses. I was regularly reading about men between the ages of 35 and 40 years old. When I was getting close to the end of my 20 days, I saw Martin's profile photo. Even though his profile was one of many amongst the masses, and I saw that he looked younger than me, I felt compelled to contact him. He replied to me. But my time was about to expire, so I gave him my email address and asked him if he would like to carry on emailing me because my subscription with that website was due to end. He started emailing me and we carried on communicating with each other that way for a while. I eventually gave him my phone number and soon he started to call me every night around 10pm, after work. The more we talked over the phone and shared our lives, the more we enjoyed each other. We used to laugh a lot, it was nice spending time with him over the phone every night. In May 2003, he came to Bolton for a weekend and we met face to face for the first time. I was pleasantly surprised; he was exactly how I would have wished my future husband to look if could have chosen. But because of my age I would not dare to have a wish list, I wasn't young enough to be fussy about people's appearance and as we get more mature, we realise that this is the least important aspect to consider about someone. So, I asked God for an honest, hardworking Christian man, preferably my age or older than me, not younger. Well, about the age… he eventually told me in one of our phone conversations, and it certainly took me a while to get used to, that he was 3 years younger than me. Again, there are other things more important to consider about a person, age is down the list. It is important to learn to compromise, not everything in life is as we wish it anyway and I had to learn that. He has dark blond hair, blue eyes, and is taller and stronger than me. He used to do weightlifting, so has very wide shoulders and strong arms. I loved the way he looked. We had a lovely weekend together that first weekend, and everybody liked him. He is very shy but has got lovely eyes and we can see in them the lovely man he is. We carried on talking over the phone after he returned to his home and three weeks later he ended the relationship with me because of the distance, he perceived the 3-hour journey as too difficult. It was painful, I was so disappointed that I had a high temperature, but it did not stop me from having joy in my Lord.

In September 2003 he came to visit me again as a friend. One week later, I sent him a letter saying that I would like to try again with him as a boyfriend and I did not need another friend, I already had plenty. I did that because I was finding it hard to move on and to feel free to try to find someone else. In my mind it was unfinished business, for me personally. In November 2003 he came to see me to tell me in person that he just wanted to be my friend. But instead, he found himself not being able to resist me and instead asked me to be his girlfriend with marriage in mind! He wanted a relationship with purpose, like me, he wanted to settle down. He came back in December and took me back to his home to meet his family.

It was lovely meeting with his parents. Val and Les are amazing and they love Jesus. Val is as sweet as my mum; it is just impossible not to love her. Les is lovable, caring and likes hugging people just like the Brazilians do. I loved them from the beginning, they are like my parents. I feel so blessed for having them as my parents in law.

Do you remember the prophecy back in January that year? It said:

> *"By the end of the year you are going to have the desire of your heart."*

There I was, with my future new family having Christmas dinner in my in-laws' house. I also met all the rest of his family during the time I spent with him that Christmas.

God wants me to enjoy Him in any situation, because in the middle of the challenge He allowed in my life, He is also waiting to use that situation to bless me and grow me. God wants me to know that He is good, his love endures forever and this must be the only thing that should matter to me.

God is good and his love endures forever.

CHAPTER 8

THE MIRACLE WEDDING

In January 2004 Martin and I bought our flight ticket to go to Brazil to see my family at Easter. I wanted them to meet Martin, my lovely boyfriend, the shortness of time that we had been together didn't matter because we were both adults, mature and we were sure about what we wanted. Our relationship was getting serious and I really wanted my family to get to know the man God had brought into my life. In February 2004, on the 15th, the day after Valentine's Day, he asked me to marry him. Again, I was not expecting that, and he was quite shy when he proposed. He had to repeat the question because I could not understand that he was proposing to me! After the third time, it clicked, I stopped, I looked at him and I understood he was asking me to marry him. Then, I said a big, fat "YES!"

He rang his parents to tell them, they were both very happy. I looked at him and I asked if he had any date in mind and he said September. My birthday is in September, in other circumstances I would love to get married in September, but we needed to be practical. So, I said: "Do you realise, if we get married when we are in Brazil in April, we will save at least the tickets to go back to Brazil in September?"

He looked at me and said: "Let's do it. Let's get married in April."

"I was just thinking that there are in fact only 6 weeks to go before our trip!"

"Let's do it. I will give you what money I have, and we do it."

He had £1500 and I had only £200 to spend on our holiday in Brazil. So, it was £1700 pounds to organise three weddings in three different cities, in two different countries and two different continents. It sounded crazy. You could think this is mad and yes, it was mad for us, but it wasn't for God. He is the God of impossible things.

Psalm 37:5 says:

> *"Commit your way to the Lord; trust Him and He will do this"*

I did not stop to do the maths; I was tired of fighting against God's will and I decided to totally trust Him. I felt in my heart that Martin was the man God had for me, this was His will for me. My parents, as I said in the first part of this book, lost nearly everything they had. They could not help me, but I was certain that God would provide everything we needed, and my job was to trust Him and to rest on Him.

So, I started making calls, I had only six weeks to organise three weddings with very little money. Let me explain the reason for three weddings: It was very important to me to get married with my parents attending because they would not be able to come over to the UK. They didn't have the money. We were planning a church wedding in Brazil, in my church over there, for my family and friends. Martin really wanted the civil ceremony to be in Yate, South Gloucestershire. This is his area, where his family and friends live, and it would constitute our second wedding. My church in Bolton wanted my wedding to be there too, at the end of the day, I was a missionary in that church. So, we had a third wedding there.

Having three weddings meant we would be able to honour everybody, they would be happy and we could start our journey together as a couple and I could carry on my journey in fulfilling God's purpose for my life with my husband. I really needed a miracle. I could not do it by myself and with so little money. I had to trust in the Lord not just because of the money, but I really needed help to pull it off. I had to trust that God was going to move things in our favour and bring the right people to help us.

Do you remember in chapter 3 when I mentioned Psalm 23:1 and I could not understand it? Well, the time to learn to understand that verse had come. When I was around 27 years old, my home group leader, Lazaro, told me once when I was very sad and confused at that time: "Silesia, I feel in my heart that you need to understand Psalm 23:1, read it in a loud voice." Then I read:

"The Lord is my shepherd, I lack nothing."

At that time, I just could not understand the application of that scripture for me, as I felt I lacked so much, because I was only looking at the circumstances surrounding me. Well, this time round, ten years later, I was in a different situation and now I could understand this verse. I was so busy working, studying, organising my trip to Brazil and our wedding that I did not have time to think and to look at the circumstances around me. I was so happy, so in love and with so much on my mind that I had to rely on God. He showed me the meaning of this verse by moving people and everything we needed in our favour, I lacked nothing at all. I dreamed about feeling special, like a princess, and I really wanted to feel the Holy Spirit's anointing on our wedding. I really wished to see people clapping hands, singing, smiling and crying because of the Holy Spirit's presence. I wanted that badly!

Please read what happened carefully, I really hope I will be able to express myself well through the words in this book, because it was amazing, a miracle what God did in my life.

PREPARING THE WEDDING

Well, I started making calls to organise the weddings in Brazil and in England when I was still in Bolton. Martin was organising the civil wedding in Yate.

Each call had a surprise prepared by God for me and assurance from Him that I was going to lack nothing. He was going to give me the desires of my heart, ranging from the way Martin looked, to a family of my dreams. I know Martin's looks are not important, but what really amazed me was the fact that God is a God of details. I never asked Him for a man with dark blonde straight hair, with blue eyes, but God knew my heart and the fact that I always found those features in a man attractive. I know it seems silly because it is who he is that really matters, but God's attention to detail really moved me. I was so confident that God was going to take care of everything else. He knew my heart and how I wanted my wedding. I just had to rely on Him, totally. I didn't have enough money or enough time for my weddings, but as I said before, the wonderful surprises started to roll in.

THE CIVIL WEDDING IN ENGLAND

Martin's parents offered to pay for the reception for the civil wedding, as a wedding gift, for around 30 people to include family and our very close friends. Amazing! Martin's brother, Andrew and his wife Tracey, helped to organise the reception at their parents' house.

When I was in Brazil preparing the church wedding, my dear friend Merilucia took me to an expensive and exclusive shop and said, "Silesia choose the dress you want for your civil wedding ceremony and I will give you it as my wedding gift."

"Are you sure Meri? This shop is so expensive."

She responded by saying she wanted me to have the best. God bless you, my friend! It was a beautiful red dress which I love. Martin's best man and his wife took the pictures of our civil wedding and gave them to us as their present. God was really providing everything through family and friends. It is amazing what we can experience when we decide to trust God and let Him do what is necessary so we can accomplish and fulfil His purpose in our lives. So, the civil wedding was sorted.

CHURCH WEDDING IN BRAZIL

When I was still in Bolton, before I left to go to Brazil, I rang my friend Evaldo to order my Brazilian invitations. Over there they are personalised, you choose the design and order them. They can go from ordinary to luxurious or even outrageously extravagant!

When I managed to talk to my friend to order our invitations for the Brazilian ceremony, his reply over the phone was: "Silesia, you can choose the invitations you want free of charge. It is my wedding gift to you." In my heart I wanted ordinary invitations as that would suit me better. I was over the moon, feeling so grateful. Tick, wedding invitations sorted.

Then I rang the wedding decorator and she said: "I will charge you the cost of the flowers and give you 50% discount off my work. It is my wedding gift to you." But she did a lot more than we had agreed. On the wedding day, I was waiting in the car before going inside the church and some friends ran towards the car to tell me that the decorator did a lot more than I had paid for. According to them, the church looked like a fairy tale. She used fabrics to give the cement brick walls a cosier feeling, to give a fairy tale feeling. The building was quite rustic and cold on its own, it had straight lines and no features. She made a lot of effort to give it a warm feeling and she achieved it. It was beautiful! She also did the reception hall, each table had flowers, the table where the cake was placed and the table where the food was served were beautifully decorated. She did an amazing job and I praised the Lord for her life.

I rang a friend, Juliet, who used to run a restaurant and a training centre to prepare young people from disadvantaged backgrounds to work in this industry. She did this wonderful work over there for over 10 years. She is an English lady, and she is back in the UK with her lovely Brazilian husband. I asked if her training centre could organise the reception for my wedding and how much it would cost. Then, she said: "Silesia, I would like to give you the reception as a wedding gift." Astonished, I replied, "But Juliet, it is a party for 200 people. It will be a lot and very expensive."

"I want to give you that. It is my gift to you."

Even more surprising is that her chef, Sr Lazaro, did not charge for his work and cooked for my wedding as a gift. And it doesn't stop here, a few days later, she came back to me to tell me about her mum, an English lady I had never met her mum before; she had sent money to cover all the costs for cutlery, tablecloths, tables and chairs for the reception. It was her mum's wedding gift to me!

It is amazing how God moves people, even people we don't know, to help us to achieve our goals when we are in the centre of God's will.

The church and decoration of the reception in Brazil were sorted. I still was running around trying to get everything else done, making decisions about service, cloths and other details. God was moving people to help me, like my dear friend Julie who lent me her car while she was at work, so that I could get to places on time and be more effective. One day, my dear Dona Rute rang me and asked me: "Silesia, where is the wedding reception going to be?"

"At the Medical Association party room," I responded.

"Do not worry about your cake, I have ordered one already and I will have it delivered there for you. Don't worry about the design, trust me, it is a beautiful cake."

I did not even ask her about the colour, I was just accepting all help, gifts and trusting God. I could not do it by myself. I did not have the money or time to be fussy.

I had to totally trust in God, He knows me better than anyone else.

My dear Brazilian Pastor, Joao Thomaz, who is a doctor and the director of a hospital in Uberlandia signed a form giving me a 50% discount on the party room to help me with the wedding. So, the church and reception were sorted. I was looking for a dress, I had just 3 weeks left to find one. So, my dear friend Galba took me to her sister-in-law, Maristela's wedding dress shop. Maristela said, "You can choose any dress you want, and it is going to be my present for you in memory of Geraldo Abrao." I was so surprised! Geraldo Abrao was Galba's late husband. He was my last boss in Brazil and also a pastor, and he had sadly died only4 months after I left Brazil. I was told that he had a lot of respect for me and that he would like that idea. Then she went on to say, "You can also choose a second dress for your English wedding and I will charge you only 50% of the value, you can take it with you to England and send it back when it suits you. Do not worry about the timing." I was completely floored by her generosity. I tried a variety of luxurious dresses on but I just didn't feel myself in them. I eventually chose two dresses with more discrete and simple designs. When I put them on, I felt myself and I knew I shined. I cannot explain it in words. It was an extraordinary feeling

I realised that to feel good and happy it doesn't have to cost a lot of money, sometimes simple things in life can be enough.

A group from my British church were in Brazil with Neneta, my pastor's wife, on a missionary trip and it was around the time of our wedding. The group was on my guest list and I was thrilled to have them and for them to make time in their busy diary to attend my wedding. Neneta gave me an envelope a few days before the wedding and when I opened it there was money inside. It was sent by my dear friend Debora who raised the money with the students and the church in Bolton, to pay for our Brazilian photographer.

They wanted to give us the wedding pictures as a gift, a very expensive present in Brazil. Neneta recommended the photographer from her niece's wedding, who was just starting his business. Because of that, he had space in his diary and he was reasonably priced, on top of being a good professional. The money in the envelope was enough to pay for the photographer she recommended. Praise the Lord for that, it is a beautiful memory which allows me to always look at re remember all the blessings we went through in that wonderful moment in our lives.

Some dear friends, like Cleria, Julie and others gave us money for our honeymoon. My dear friend Enock, who is a dentist, gave me some cosmetic work on my teeth to improve their appearance to look good in the photos.

Our wedding was on a Sunday morning in the small Sal da Terra church in the Vigilato Pereira area, which was big enough for around 250 people. The main church where I used to go was too big, its capacity was for more than a thousand people. My friend Kellen advised me to go for a smaller church, which would give the feeling of cosiness and warmth. I am happy I listened to her advice and went for the smaller church. I used to go to this church in Vigilato Pereira for around 2 years when I was in my late twenties until the main church called me back to lead the drama group. Pastor Helder was the leader there. He was a pastor of love and a paediatrician whose legacy impacted many families in Uberlandia city. He was well known for his love, faithfulness and dedication as a pastor and a children's doctor. When I told him about my plans to get married in his church, he immediately cancelled their Sunday morning service for us. What a lovely memory he left in my life when he passed away more recently.

I booked the hairdresser and again, they charged me fifty percent less than other shops asked me for the event and they also gave me a skin treatment and did my eyelashes for free. And what's more, I was the only person in that salon on that Sunday morning and I was treated like a princess, they certainly gave me more than I paid for! The blessings abounded. This is what God does for us, he treats us like royal children and moves the world around us, moving even people we don't know. Businesses forget their profit margin when God orders them to be an instrument to help us to fulfil God's purpose.

It is amazing what and who God can use to bless us and shine His glory through our lives.

My friends Vanderley and Cristina (she is the lady who God used to reveal to me that I was going to have a child of my own flesh and blood), drove me in their car and lent me their house to have our wedding pictures taken there. My friend Kleber and his family looked after Martin the night before our wedding because my house was full of visitors, my relatives from Patos de Minas city came for our wedding and stayed in my house. There were more than 20 people in that small three-bedroomed house and it would be too much for Martin to cope with.

MORE THAN A HEN PARTY, IT WAS A NIGHT OF REVELATION

Kellen, my friend who advised me to book a smaller church, organised a hen party for me at her house. I made only one cake for this party, while Kellen and our friends took care of everything else. It was a lovely night, how nice it was to see so many friends together again, to catch up and to share with them that moment that was so special in my life, to have fun and just enjoy each other's company. They had known me for a long time and I knew how happy they were for me. People came and brought me shoes, intimate clothing, toiletries, make up, perfume, bags, and jewellery. All of them very useful in the new chapter of my life. There were ladies that brought encouraging messages to help me in my new journey as a wife. They were all very important, but I must mention people whose words touched me deeply. One was from Pastor Fabiana Bastos, she said:

> *"Silesia, always be your husband's best friend, in another words, always choose him to spend time with and to share your problems, dreams and plans with."*

I never forgot these words and in times of storm in my marriage, I always remember these words and I remind myself that Martin is my best friend and it is always worth investing in him.

Another thing happened at my hen party which really surprised me. My mum asked to speak and she told us something that was new to me. She said: "My husband and I always wanted a girl and when Silesia was born and the midwife put her in my arms, I was so happy. I was holding my little girl and the first thing I did was to lift her very high to thank God and to give her back to Him. I asked Him to guide her, to keep her safe and to let me look after her for Him." I was very surprised listening to her. My mum had no idea what sharing that did for me, the impact that action caused in my life. She was a Christian at the time of my hen party, she became a Christian after me, but when I was born she wasn't a church-going person, she had never been taught about the bible like lots of other Brazilians.

At that moment, she was dedicating me to God with no knowledge about it.

She told us that she asked God to take me back as His daughter and she was just going to look after me for Him. She asked Him to keep me safe and guide me throughout my life.

I understood at that moment why God started to speak to me at the age of 6 years old and why I have always listened to His voice guiding me in every big decision I have to make in my life. I was very moved hearing my mum's story and I was very grateful she did that for me. That was the best present she could have given to me. It is just a shame she is not here with us to read this book. She went back home to heaven in April 2019.

WEDDING DAY IN BRAZIL

The wedding in Brazil was beautiful, the church was full of people and the decorations were wonderful. My friend Sara and the church band made a huge effort to give the best they could and for that they rehearsed. For my entrance I chose Agnus Dei in Portuguese. I entered the church accompanied by my father, I felt the Holy Spirit's presence strongly as I was walking down the aisle with my dad by my side. The anointing was so strong that people started to clap as we were passing by them and some of them were crying. That was a dream come true, I wanted that so much, I wanted the anointing of God to fill the whole place and to touch everybody there. I was so happy. I could not cry because I could not stop smiling. That moment in that church felt like a fairy tale and I was the princess in this story. My friends from the band prepared one special song in English especially for my husband. That really meant a lot to me. They took time to learn and practice a song in a foreign language to please us, instead of doing their own thing. The worship in general was amazing, the preach was a real blessing. The service was lovely, emotional and anointed by the Holy Spirit.

I really appreciate what all my friends did and I am so grateful. Pastor Cesar stood by Martin's side to translate for him during the ceremony and to translate the preaching done by Steve, one of the leaders from my English church, to the Portuguese in the church done. Gilberto, my dear pastor for years in Brazil was by his side and lead the vows. When it was my turn to say my vows, I opened the bible in Ruth 1:16-17.

> *"But Ruth replied, 'Don't urge me to leave you or to turn back from you. Where you go, I will go, and where you stay, I will stay. Your people will be my people and your God my God. Where you die, I will die, and there I will be buried. May the Lord deal with me, be it ever so severely, if even death separates you and me.'"*

In fact, I felt in my heart that this is what I was doing, I was leaving my country, and everything I loved about it; the language, culture, my family and friends , all in order to follow Martin and to serve the Lord with him in a foreign land. My wish is to grow old together, fulfilling God's purpose for my life and now for our lives too. At the end of the day, after we became one, our lives also became one and my purpose joins God's purpose for him in some point of our lives, though other parts of our purpose do remain individual, as we are individuals. We cannot forget that we are unique and we are accountable to deal with our walk with God individually. My faith journey is between God and I. But I need Martin by my side, to be part of my journey with God, and I to be part of his journey.

Everybody who attended the church service was invited to the reception. When we got there, I was pleasantly surprised. The party room looked amazing; the cake was wonderful, perfect. The food cooked by Mr. Lazaro was amazing, and the tables were well decorated. The waiters were so polite and kind. There was not another word to describe the event but perfection. We took our honeymoon in Caldas Novas which is a spring water area with a beautiful water park, nothing in England compares to this water park over there. We had a magical time.

WEDDING DAY IN THE UK

Back in England, our civil wedding in Yate and our reception at my parents in law's house were lovely. A couple of days after the civil wedding I went back to Bolton to train someone to replace me and to organise our wedding there. Again, God was showing me that I will lack nothing in every aspect of my life because He is my shepherd.

The church in Bolton gave us the use of the wedding venue as a gift. We just bought the supplies for the food, cake and some decorations; and various friends got together to organise everything for us.

My dear friend Nara could not go to our wedding but stayed up until late the night before making us a lovely and delicious Brazilian wedding cake as a gift. Another friend, Marjorie, made the bridesmaid dress free of charge.

Tia Rute, the lady who gave us the cake in Brazil, was in Bolton and she prepared the flowers, my bouquet and she did my hair. Neneta and other friends prepared and decorated the church and party room.

My dear friend Leila and another friend cooked the meal free of charge as a gift.

Luciana and Mark gave us the wedding pictures as a present. Mark's hobby is taking pictures and he did a great job.

Pedro Paulo drove me to church. Other friends helped a lot with washing up and tidying up.

After finishing the wedding, I saw something that really moved me. The person we hired to wash the dishes left before he'd finished. So, Pastor Marcos rolled up his beautiful shirt sleeves and washed the pans. The next thing Neneta and other friends helped too, they tidied everything up before leaving the venue. I am so grateful for my friends who always stand by my side.

May God bless you all always for all the hard work and effort in making this moment, a time to be remembered forever. There was so much love, humility, commitment, integrity, perseverance in giving us another perfect wedding.

Martin and I were so happy and feeling so loved that nothing would take our peace away, even the fact that our car broke down and we had to leave Bolton in an AA truck, with our car on the back, to come to Bristol. We told the driver that we had just left our wedding, which had us all laughing together. A funny moment to be remembered forever. It was fun.

This is my opportunity to say thanks to everybody for everything. I am sorry if I forgot someone, I really tried hard to remember everything, but seventeen years have already gone and it is not easy to remember all the details.

CHAPTER 9

MY PURPOSE WAS BECOMING CLEARER

"If you are willing and obedient, you will eat the good things of the land."-Isaiah 1:19 (NIV)

UNDERSTANDING GOD'S PURPOSE FOR HUMANKIND

I mentioned Isaiah 1:19 earlier in the book as it was really becoming a reality in my life and continues to impact my life regularly. I am a work in progress in God's hands, we all are, and I hope that as I share my learnings that you too will be blessed . The truth about this verse is that it is not a statement of trade; it is not an exchange that God is offering us. Pastor Paulo Borges Junior from Sal da Terra church in Goiania city clarified this concept for me so well during one of his social media teachings. John 3:1-15 tells the story of Nicodemus who asked Jesus how someone can enter the kingdom of God, and then he asked how a grown person could be born again if it is not possible to go back into the mother's womb?

It is very important we understand that lack of faith is linked to the fact that we resist interpreting the bible according to the Holy

Spirit's guidance. We cannot rely on our own understanding which is limited by our brain's capacity and we can even sometimes interpret scripture according to our own interests.

On the other hand, the Holy Spirit gives us a supernatural interpretation of the word of God which goes beyond our human understanding and interprets it according to God's will.

God's purpose is for His children to learn to live as a family, to develop communion and relationship with each other and with Him.

He wants us to be transformed in our understanding and to become a better version of ourselves to be able to communicate His virtues to other people around us; virtues of love, compassion, kindness, respect, forgiveness, patience, self-control, resilience, honesty, sincerity, and the list goes on.

The more I give from myself, the more I become empty of my own desires and of my will. This will create a bigger space inside me which can be filled with knowledge about God and by getting close to Him it will bring more balance in my life and help me to feel good about myself.

Jesus came as a human not to tell us what to do, but He came as a human, in the form of Jesus, to show us how to be the son of God just as Christ on the cross was.

We are called to live a life like Jesus and to become Christlike.

We need to understand that salvation is not a destination point.

Salvation is a process of transformation and fulfilment of God's purpose in our lives daily.

As we grow in knowledge about God our minds are transformed, our attitudes changed, we get closer and more intimate with God. Our lives move in line with His will and we become happier, well resolved, well established as a person, independent of circumstances around us. Consequently, we will better communicate God's virtue through our lives, be an inspiration for other people to follow who might start seeking transformation in their own lives too.

So, remember, Heaven is our home, it is where we will go after we fulfil our purpose on earth.

UNDERSTANDING GOD'S PURPOSE FOR MY LIFE

1 Corinthians 10:13:

> *"No temptation has overtaken you except what is common to mankind. And God is faithful; he will not let you be tempted beyond what you can bear. But when you are tempted, he will also provide a way out so that you can endure it."*

Romans 8:28:

> *"And we know that in all things God works for the good of those who love Him, who have been called according to His purpose."*

All that God wanted from me was and always will be to have a close relationship with Him. He wants me to trust Him in any circumstance, no matter what, like toddlers trust their parents. By trusting Him I open my heart up and start living a life in line with His will. My will is becoming more and more in line with His will. And it is great, really!

God doesn't make us do things, but He shows us what's best for us and we feel good, fulfilled when we obey Him, because His plan for us is far, far better than our plans for our lives.

God sees the whole picture for humankind, we only see immediately around us. So, we have a part to play in this big plan God has for His creation. I need to figure out my part in this plan and give my best and always trust God.

Because I am obeying God, it doesn't mean it will be easy, that I won't go through difficult times, but I know for sure that God has got a purpose in everything that happens to me and I must just trust His judgements and His choices. Everything will be fine in the end because God will not allow anything to happen in my life which is more than I can cope with. I need to learn to live one day at a time, without anxiety, just trusting God.

MY MARRIED LIFE

I have no shadow of a doubt that Martin is the man God has set apart for me. We got married when I was 37 years old and my biological clock was close to its final point. It used to worry me, so I wanted to try for a baby 6 months after our wedding. Martin said no to me because he needed more time. I was very sad because of that and I used to cry a lot. For a moment I forgot God's prophecies for my life, again I started to look at circumstances around me, in this case it was my age and it brought me a lot of pain. I needed to learn to wait and to trust God in all circumstances. Today I understand his reaction, and he was right. We really needed time to get to know each other first before bringing a vulnerable little person into our lives. In fact, we used to live in different cities and because of that, we didn't have a close relationship and we didn't have a lot of face-to-face contact. We used to talk everyday over the phone, but relationship is more than just that, there are habits, culture, language, environment, and physical aspects that need to be taken into consideration and we didn't have the opportunity to cover that before our wedding. Just because Martin is my perfect match it doesn't mean we have a perfect marriage. We went through challenges in the first years of our journey together. At the end of the day, we were brought up in two very different cultures, backgrounds, and languages. My English had improved since I left Brazil, but it was still poor compared to today. Many times, my husband had to repeat himself several times until I asked him to use other vocabulary, simpler, with no expressions which I used to find hard to understand, it was stressful for him. One day he asked me if the pasta was running out, I looked at him like a little girl, I could not understand what he meant and I kept asking him to repeat himself which he did, four times! In my mind running was just used to express when someone was exercising, literally running. It is normal for a couple to have a time of adjusting to their new lives, but in cases like ours where the individuals are from different countries they have even more adjustments to consider.

In November 2005 I was in church and a friend of mine, who was heavily pregnant, came to me and told me she would like to pray for me. After she prayed, she said that she was feeling in her heart that by next Christmas, in 2006, I was going to have my child in my arms. I received that prayer and kept it in my heart. I wanted to be a mum so badly!

When he felt ready, in January 2006, Martin said yes, I could stop taking the pill and we could try to have a baby. Our first child was born in December 2006, a little boy who we call Joao-Lucas. He was supposed to born in January 2007, but to do as He had promised me the year before, Joao-Lucas sat in my womb in a very dangerous position. I had a scan done on December 19th and the doctor told me to stay in hospital over Christmas and New Year until I started having contractions, because if my waters had broken when I was at home it could cause brain damage to Joao-Lucas. Martin asked if he could be delivered by C-section as soon as possible. The doctor said yes, the baby was ready and he booked me for a C-section which I had done on 21 December. I prayed beforehand asking God to give me a supernatural delivery time with no pain. I was very scared of the pain. So, I had a C-section done because he was in this funny bridge position and I never had any contractions.

Martin was with me in the theatre and I was kept awake. When Joao-Lucas was brought out of my tummy and was cleaned up they gave him to Martin to hold him. Instantly Martin's eyes welled up when he held his son for the first time and together, at that moment, while the doctors were stitching my tummy up, we repeated my mum's actions. We prayed, as parents, offering our baby back to God, asking Him to guide him, to protect him and to allow us to look after him. When we were praying, the nurses stopped working and were watching us. Some of them were moved and one Christian nurse told us afterwards how moved she was and she felt God's anointing. Later we also took him in front of the church and dedicated him to God.

The next morning when the doctor came to visit me, I was already sitting up in bed putting lipstick on. She was very surprised. The day after that, I was discharged from hospital and we had Christmas with our son on Monday, 25December like the prophecy I had received the year before. Since birth Joao-Lucas has been adorable, very calm, well behaved, sensitive, responsible and considerate. I praise the Lord for our beautiful son whose name Joao means *God is gracious with me*. Two prophecies came true in my life, I had a child of my flesh and blood, and God was answering the prophecy my friend shared with me a year ago. Thanks to my Lord for all His faithfulness, love and care for my family and me. It was peaceful in our house; I was so happy to be a wife and a mum but I still felt in my heart that our family was not complete yet.

BECOMING FOSTER CARERS

After Joao-Lucas turned one, we started to try for another child and I couldn't get pregnant easily, so I went to see the doctor. They did a fertility test and it turned out that there wasn't any treatment to offer me as I was fertile, there was nothing wrong with me. Immediately I remembered God's revelation when I was 18 years old that I was going to adopt children. I didn't feel sad for not falling pregnant; God brought peace into my heart and I understood immediately that Joao-Lucas was going to be our only biological child and we were going to have adopted children. This process of having more children was more painful that I could imagine, but it wasn't more than we could cope with because this part of God's plan was for the whole family and not just for me as I used to think when I was a single lady. So, if that message was really coming from God, it would become true but it doesn't mean it would be easy. In my life, I have been experiencing that each step I move forward there is a cost and often there have been tears along the way. I decided to talk to Martin about the possibility of adoption, I had a lot of love inside of me to share, and I was longing for more children. But to my surprise his answer was, "No, I cannot love other people's children as my own, any baby we have needs to be from my flesh and blood." I was devastated but I had it in my heart that our relationship was more important, at the end of the day I was a mum. I wasn't going to force him into it, if it was God's will for that to happen, for us to adopt a child, He was going to bring the child to us. I badly wanted at least another one, but not at the cost of Martin's suffering.

God's way of working always exceeds our understanding and all things happen for our own good.

At that time, the Baby P case was all the over the news on most television channels., I used to look at Joao-Lucas, who was the same age as Baby P, and wondered how a mum and her boyfriend could be so evil and torture that little boy to death? My heart was so moved, I was so distressed with the case and it made me cry a lot. The desire of my heart at that moment was to bring all the children in risky situations into my home to protect them. I talked to Martin about this and asked him if he would agree to become a foster carer, that way I could have more children to look after and to share my love with, and the money we would receive from this work would help him to pay for our monthly expenses. It would allow me to stay at home, look after our son and earn some money to help with our living costs and I would have more children. Everybody would be happy.

Martin agreed to that and we started the process to become foster carers which took a year to be finalised, in November 2009. During the process, the social worker told us that we were not allowed to adopt as we were being trained to be foster carers and not adoptive parents. We said it was fine with us. After finishing the process, we were transferred to another department and we had a different social worker to deal with, we were now officially foster carers and we were on the list waiting for the right child to come along. In the

South West, the shortage of foster carers was quite substantial and it brought us hope to get a child as quickly as possible. Joao-Lucas turned 3 in December yet there were no more children at that point. At the end of January we were still waiting and Andrea, our social worker, came to our home for a visit. I asked her the reason it was taking so long if they were in so much need of foster carers. It just didn't make sense! She told me it wasn't personal, there was nothing wrong with us, but they needed to match families and there was not a good match for us yet. Then, I told her that if there were twins, I would love to look after them. She looked at me very surprised and asked if I was sure about that. I said "yes, I would love to look after twins." In March she came back to us to tell us that they were considering us for one set of twin girls and I very quickly answered, "Yes please, we want them." She said "wait, it is complicated."

According to her, they were girls, born in February at 27 weeks, very premature babies and because of that, the placement had to be perfect. The girls were extremely vulnerable and needed a qualified carer. I knew I could do that. In my heart I was sure about having them and peace filled me. She asked me to talk to Martin about that. When Martin came back home in the evening, I told him about the twins and immediately he said yes, he wanted them. It was amazing how things were falling into place like a big puzzle.

God is amazing and we cannot imagine what He can do in our lives and through our lives when we put ourselves in the centre of His will, in obedience to His voice.

CHAPTER 10

GOD'S PLANS GO BEYOND
OUR UNDERSTANDING

God's plans go beyond our comprehension, so don't try to understand, only trust Him! (Alice Rodrigues)

GOING THROUGH THE STORM

In March 2010 we went to hospital to start having contact with the twin girls at the NICU, at the age of seven weeks. When we got there, it was very emotional, they were tiny, Mia was 2.2 pounds and Maisie was 2 pounds. When Martin picked one of the girls up in his arms his eyes misted up, he had the same reaction when he was holding Joao-Lucas in the theatre soon after he was cleaned up. I felt that he was fathering the girls right there in his first contact with them, it looked like he had forgotten that they were not his flesh and blood, he was completely in love with them. I asked him to protect his heart because the girls were supposed to come to us for just 6 months and I didn't want to see him heartbroken. I was also in love with the girls, but I was reminding myself all the time that they would only be with us for a short time.

Now I understood why Social Services couldn't find a match for us before, despite the shortage of foster cares in the South West. The girls' biological mum found out about her pregnancy in November when we became qualified, and the twins were only born at twenty-seven weeks in February, and they were discharged nine weeks later. They were supposed to come to us, so God closed the door to allow any other child to be matched with us.

Just because I was fulfilling God's purpose for my life didn't mean it was going to be easy. Once again, I found myself going through a storm and it reminded me of the passage in Matthew 14:23-31 which says:

> *"When Jesus dismissed the people, he went up alone to a mountain to pray. Later that night, he was there alone, and the boat was already at a considerable distance from the land, battered by the waves because the wind was blowing against him.*
>
> *Shortly before dawn, Jesus went out to them, walking on the water. When the disciples saw him walking on the sea, they were terrified. 'It is a ghost!' they said and they cried out in fear. But Jesus immediately said to them, 'Courage! That's me. Don't be afraid!'"*
>
> *'Lord,' Peter said, 'if it is you, send me to meet you over the waters.'*
>
> *'Come,' he answered.*
>
> *Then Peter got off the boat, walked on the waters, and went toward Jesus. But when he noticed the wind, he was afraid, and began to sink, he cried, 'Lord, save me!'*

> *Immediately Jesus reached out and held him. And he said, 'Man of little faith, why did you doubt it?'"*

The disciples were going through a storm in the sea and this can be a frightening situation to be in. We all have different types of storms in our lives, only you can identify those in your life. What are the waves that have been flung against your boat? Are they depression, death, anxiety, issues with finances, relationships, or children? Honestly, whatever the storm, it is very hard to get through it and sometimes it can even bring a feeling of abandonment. The strong wind can blind us and make us feel lost. But the message I would like to share with you is that in any circumstances we find ourselves in, God is with us, God does not abandon us. He is the provider of everything, and He has provided everything we need. When we understand that we can go through the storm feeling calm and safe and certain that God never abandons us, then this certainty brings comfort to our heart. God is good, God is complete and He has a purpose in everything He allows in our lives.

Remember that when Peter got out that boat and was watching Jesus and trusting Him for this miracle, he too could walk on water, but when he got distracted and focussed on the circumstances, he sank. Jesus wanted to bless him with this miracle, but He needed Peter to have his eyes on Him, right throughout.

When we are in the middle of a storm it is necessary to look at Jesus all the time. We can't look at the circumstances around us, even if it looks like there is no solution and there is no hope. We must keep strong, focus and fix our eyes on the author and finisher of our faith, Jesus.

I had shared earlier that God brought me to England as a missionary, He taught me that my happiness comes from him, regardless of my situation. This means that it doesn't matter what circumstances I am in, my favourite place needs to always be the centre of God's will. It is there where I have joy in the Lord and I am developing my life with purpose.

Bear in mind something very important, God never promised me that it would be easy and that I would not have a hard time. What God promised me is that He will never forsake me and that He will help me to go through every storm I have in my journey safely.

WE LIVED A MIRACLE

Mia and Maisie were in the NICU until they were nine weeks old, when they reached the minimum weight of just over four pounds. We were able to visit them and take care of them in their last two weeks in NICU. Before they were discharged from the hospital, the doctors insisted that Martin and I do the resuscitation training just in case we needed it to help them. They were perfect on the outside; beautiful, blonde, blue eyes, but they were not fully formed inside yet. Both of their lungs were still not completely formed and Maisie's heart had a hole in it. They were very fragile and needed a lot of care and complete attention, it was a lot of work bearing in mind that all the hard work came twice as much, at the end of the day there were two of them and we also had a three-year-old boy.

The day we went to pick them up in the maternity ward was a very special day for us. We were very happy and very proud, each one of us was carrying a car seat to bring them home. It looked like we were the parents already. Everything was going well until one day, three weeks later, on Thursday, 6 May 2010 after I had picked them up from a contact session with their biological mother. I was driving back home and I had our three children in the car. Her home was only a four-minute drive from us, but because they were very vulnerable, and England is a cold country we were advised not to expose them unnecessarily to the cold. I used to drive everywhere to keep them warm. Well, when we got home, I parked the car outside the front door, I had a van with a sliding door. I opened the van door to get the children out of the car. Next to the door on the passenger side there was no seat inside the van. It was easier for me to access the back row to put the seat belt on Joao-Lucas and it was easier to get the children out of the car. There were three rows of seats in the van and the girls used to go on the middle row which had two seats.

Mia was the one on the first seat this time. When I got her car seat out and looked at her face, I was shocked. I realised she was lifeless, blue. I looked around looking for help, I took her out of the car seat and I put her on the van floor, checked her breathing; nothing. I looked around for help and I noticed that my next-door neighbour was putting rubbish in the black bin, so, I ran to him in desperation. In my despair I spoke to him in Portuguese, I was screaming, asking him to call the ambulance. He looked at me and, clearly, he couldn't understand a word of what I was saying, but my distress made him go after me when I was running back to the car. Then, I repeated in English, "please call an ambulance." For seconds he was transfixed at that scene before he realised it was a scary situation. I was doing CPR on her. He went back to call the ambulance and came back with his wife. When they got close to the car, I was pressing her little chest, using two of my fingers, she was just three and a half months old. The ambulance was quick, but at that moment every second counted and it felt like an eternity.

When I was looked at my daughter lying on the ground, lifeless, dead, I didn't even think about the circumstance, I didn't have time for that, I was too busy trying to keep my focus on Jesus. He was the only one that could do something for Mia at that moment, there was nothing I could do apart from CPR and pray. So, I really focused on trying to do the right thing. I remember that I swallowed the crying at first, pulled myself together and I put my mouth on her little mouth and I blew air into her lungs three times. Then, I started to press two fingers against her little chest. At that moment, as I started pressing my fingers against her chest, I couldn't hold my tears back anymore, I was doing CPR, crying and praying, all at once.

> "Lord, blow life on Mia in the name of Jesus, bring her back, I'm not ready to lose my baby, help me, Lord."

I kept pressing against her little chest 30 times and then I blew air into her lungs three more times through her mouth. Praise the Lord her colour was coming back and she had returned when the paramedics arrived. Soon after this, the ambulance came back to took us to the hospital but not after I had called my in-laws who came to stay with Maisie and Joao-Lucas for me. At A&E they put us in an observation room, in fact, none of the paramedics saw her dead and for the doctors it was just a mother's report who was not a health professional. They had left us in the observation room just in case. It was a busy day as usual and they didn't bother coming to see Mia. I wasn't alone with Mia, our social worker, Andrea, came to be with me and Martin was on his way to the hospital from work, it was a long distance for him to travel and there was a lot of traffic in the city centre. I was with Mia in my arms and suddenly she began to die again and Andrea noticed and shouted for help. One doctor came and grabbed her from my arms and ran off with her towards the resuscitation room. I stood there, in the middle of the room, with my arms in the air, I was in shock. The nurse came and said to me, "Please come, I'm going to take you to your daughter." Andrea accompanied me and the nurse explained to me what was happening before opening the door to where Mia was. "Your daughter is very ill, the doctors had to resuscitate her and they're doing everything they can to help her." I walked into the room and saw our little baby girl, lying on the hospital bed and surrounded by doctors and nurses trying to save her. A few moments later Martin arrived and Andrea left, so that he could stay with me in the room. We both sat on the chair in the corner, in shock, watching the doctors and nurses fighting to keep her alive.

A doctor came to us and said, "I'm sorry, but she is dying. We collected samples to try to find out what it is killing her, but we don't have time to wait for the lab results to come back. The only chance she has got is if we inject her body with all types of antibiotics we have against bacteria and against viruses at once and hope it can kill what it is killing her." I stared at the doctor's face and tears flowed from my eyes without sobbing and I said "Please do whatever you think is necessary." I knew I didn't have parental responsibility, but they were just communicating what they were going to do, and in my heart, she was our daughter already, so I had to agree with them. I knew it was their responsibility, they had to do what they could to try to save our baby girl.

From the moment the doctors saw that it was not just a mum story, that Mia was in fact very ill, they stayed around her all the time. There were a team of around six professionals (doctors and nurses) fighting for her life for more than five hours. There was a younger doctor whose role was to keep Mia alive while the others discussed options and made decisions about what to do next.

Please remember, the fear of death is the weapon the devil uses to enslave us and take our attention away from Jesus.

I was so focused on what was happening that I did not even look at Martin and I did not even ask if he was praying. I did not want to distract myself and risk looking at the circumstances around me. I knew Mia was part of God's plans for our lives and I believe that none of God's plans are frustrated. I also didn't keep asking: "Why me Lord?" Instead of that, I asked "Why not me?"

After all, we have been given not only the privilege of living in Christ, but also, the privilege of suffering in Christ.

Later, the same doctor who had talked to me before, came back to talk to me again. She said: "She is stabilising, and we are going to transfer her to the Intensive Care Unit. You have no idea what you did, do you?" I looked at her and I was confused. She continued: "I am an Intensive Care Unit doctor and this is my everyday job, it is also part of my job description to be able to resuscitate children and I have done it many times in my life. But a few months ago, I had to do it on a close friend's child, and despite my experience, I trembled, I didn't think I could do it. You are a mum, and you are not a health care professional, yet you had the strength to help your daughter. Most parents in situations such as this panic and the child dies. They can't do what you did."

I said: "I just did what needed to be done." The tears flowed. I couldn't say a lot, I was still in shock, I had had a long and very difficult day. I was feeling drained, exhausted.

It is important that we understand that to have faith is to have sensitivity to understand our role in the moment of need.

I had to be proactive and to do something by faith and I did it trusting that God was in control of the situation, I also prayed. But there, in that room, while Mia was being assisted by professionals, my job was to pray in the spirit and to try to stay strong and that's what I did all the time.

In the name of Jesus, worry more about God's direction than about the obscurities of life (Pastor Paulo Borges Junior).

I needed God's direction, after all, I had another three-and-a-half-month-old baby and a three-year-old boy at home waiting for me. Thank God the antibiotics worked, she became stable and was taken to the Intensive Care Unit. Every morning Joao-Lucas, Maisie and I used to spend all day in the hospital with Mia. I used to take clean clothes and nappies. Martin had to go to work and I was back home in the evening with the children to make dinner, put the clothes in the wash and put the other two little ones in their beds. The following week Maisie was also admitted into hospital with a chest infection and the two of them stayed there, each one of them in their own room, but the rooms were next to each other to make it easier for me. Maisie stayed only one week. Mia stayed another week; it was three weeks in total for her. This was the first of many other trips to hospital with the girls. The neighbours got used to seeing the ambulance stop outside our house, taking me with one of the girls to the hospital. This lasted until they were around two years old when gradually, they grew out of asthma as their lungs became fully formed.

OUR TINY BABIES CONQUERED OUR HEARTS

Our social worker came to visit us as usual when Mia and Maisie turned eleven months old to tell us that the Judge decided they were going to be on the adoption list as their mum was not fit to be a mum at that time. To our surprise she asked if we had considered the possibility of adopting them because she thought it would be perfect. Wow, what a change! We were told before that adoption wasn't an option for us and now, they asked that question from out of the blue! Of course, I said yes, we have been considering that and we would like to know if we could apply. Her immediate answer was "Yes, you can, and I will bring you the form next time I come to visit you."

I told Martin when he came back home and we were so happy because our baby girls really conquered our hearts, including Joao-Lucas'. He used to cry with the possibility of the girls being taken away and he asked several times "Please mum, don't let them take the girls away, I love them." It was heart breaking to hear our three-year-old boy say that. But with this possibility it looked like we were going to complete our family and I couldn't wait to call the girls our own.

It seems that another piece of this puzzle was about to fall into place, but it didn't mean that it was going to fall into place smoothly. I will repeat again what I said before, just because I was fulfilling God's purpose for my life it doesn't mean that everything was going to be easy. Once again, I found myself going through a storm or more appropriately let's say a hurricane.

When we are in the boat with Jesus there is always resistance, but we don't need to be afraid because He will never forsake us.

I know it doesn't make the process easy but knowing this gives us confidence that we are going to be safe and everything is going to be fine in the end. The adoption process lasted nineteen months and I cried throughout the whole process. It was painful, stressful and by the end I was drained.

A few weeks after we submitted the form requesting to be the girls' adopted family, we received a visit from two social workers. They were from the adoption department and it was the first visit to start our process towards the goal to complete our family. The two ladies requested to meet with Martin and I together and so we received them into our home to listen to what they had to say. Well, the first thing they told us after introducing themselves was, "We are not going to make this easy for you two because you are the girls' foster carers. They are highly adoptable, they are blonde, have blue eyes, are girls and are babies and there will be a queue of people wanting them once we publish their picture in our magazine. Because of that we will be fussy and choose what we think is best for the girls. We are going to turn you inside out and your lives into hell." It was scary to hear that, we couldn't think of our lives without our girls, they were part of our family, they were our daughters, and the possibility of losing them would tear our hearts apart.

We were decorating our home and had just changed the carpets. The house was looking lovely, I was so happy with the result. It was two weeks after completing that the adoption team came for their first visit and they came back that week. I thought they would be happy with the clean and newly decorated house, we had finished on Monday of that week, and they came on Thursday. We received them together, Martin and I, as they requested. They had something to tell us and again, it brought sorrow to our souls. They told us that we had to move to another area, otherwise they were going to find another family elsewhere for the girls. They gave us a list of places we were not allowed to live inside a 5 miles radius.

I cried and prayed the whole weekend and we also asked the church to pray for us because we had no money at all to move. I asked God for a miracle, wisdom, direction, guidance, we needed them all. Over the weekend we were looking for houses outside our city where we could find a cheaper house that would suit our family lifestyle. On Monday, I saw a perfect house for us in a local newspaper which was around five miles away from where we used to live, but it was above our budget. It was in one area Martin and I had always wanted to live in but we had never talked about it because it was a more expensive area. Martin asked "How are we going to buy this house? We can't afford that."

I said, "God will provide the miracle as we need it." We offered a lot less than the asking price and it was accepted and God put our finances in place for us because we couldn't, it was a miracle.

It didn't stop there, the social workers turned Martin and I inside out as they said they would, I can't tell you everything that happened because it was very personal and very painful. I can tell you that they wanted to take the girls away from us and they tried to three times. When we went to the panel for the first time to be accepted as adoptive parents we were rejected because of my size. They gave me three months to lose some weight or they were going to reject us next time despite my very good medical report. Our social worker rang me when she heard the news, she couldn't believe it, she wanted to know what happened, but we couldn't explain. We thought that the love and care we were giving the girls would be enough but it turned out that, in their book, it wasn't enough, and we could not understand what they wanted. In my opinion, (maybe I am wrong because no one ever told me) it was because I wasn't thinner, younger and financially secure according to their standard. We were about to go to Brazil in December to visit my family and to take the girls before they turned two to take advantage of the cheaper flights. The stress we were under was big and instead of losing weight I went back to the panel one stone bigger. The social worker met us there and asked me "Please, don't cry this time."

I said: "Sorry, I can't help it."

At that meeting, the panel asked us the reason why we wanted to adopt the girls. I felt like I had something in my throat and I said firmly and with a strong conviction: "Because we love them, they are our daughters."

They asked what we would be prepared to do for them and I did not hesitate and with confidence I said: "I would cross the world for them if it were necessary, they are my daughters."

They asked about Joao-Lucas and if we thought that he would need some professional help because of the adoption, a therapist. I said "He will need a therapist if you take his sisters away, he cried when we told him about this possibility, and he told me that he doesn't want them to go away as he loves them."

They asked us to leave the room and we came back afterwards to a decision to allow us to adopt them. I cried intensely; I was so relieved. After this panel our social worker rang us to say congratulations and she told me they were relieved our process was heading to be finalised. She said that her team was looking forward to it ending because it was the most stressful process they had dealt with.

In August 2012 we finally had the ceremony at the court to receive the adoption certificate and to be formally and legally recognised and accepted as Mia and Maisie's parents in the eyes of the law. We were so happy; the girls were ours now and we were responsible for their wellbeing and to make decisions for them until they reach adulthood.

CHAPTER 11

GENERAL VISION OF
GOD'S PURPOSE FOR MY LIFE

In the evening after the court had finalised our girls' adoption process, I took them to bed and I prayed for them as I used to do. But that night, I felt different, I realised that I wasn't a foster mum anymore, I was their mum and I had authority over their lives, I could pray for them with authority and bless them, make choices, teach and guide them like Martin and I used to do with Joao-Lucas. On Sunday, we took them to the front of the church and we dedicated them to God just as we did with our son. We prayed and introduced them to church as our daughters. After the church service we about fifty people came back to our house, family and friends, to have lunch with us, and to celebrate that important moment with us. Our family was complete, thanks to our Lord. The last revelation from the time when I was living in Brazil which God gave to me when I was eighteen years old was complete.

Adoption is a very important step we take in life. In fact, I believe we should adopt not just children from a different family but also, we should adopt our own biological children. I believe that the reason some parents abandon, neglect or abuse their children is because they just give birth to their children, they didn't really receive them in their heart which is the place where the adopted child is formed. The adopted child is formed in our heart and the biological child is formed in our womb, but the biological child also needs to be formed in our heart. So, both types of children, adopted and biological need to have a place in our heart, we need to take responsibility for both, that way we will give them our best.

God's picture is bigger than ours, He had prepared me from a young age to be the person I am becoming today and one of the aspects of this transformation is to make a difference in Mia and Maisie's lives. God loves these girls so much that He prepared, trained and brought me from Brazil to be their mum. If I had refused to come, He would had given this privilege to another family and I would have missed the opportunity to be an instrument in God's hands to bless our girls and my husband. I would have missed the opportunity to be a fulfilled person and to live a life with purpose. I would have missed the opportunity to be a complete and happy person and my son, this lovely and beautiful human being, would not exist.

God moved everything that was needed to help me to accomplish my purpose, we still don't have an abundance of money, our finances are always tight, but God has always moved people to bless us at the right time. God has blessed us with a lovely family home in a desirable area, with a good school, so we could be instruments in His hands to bless our children and give our best to them.

I have learnt to stop complaining when things are taking longer than I expected or when my plans have changed. I always try to remember that God has got a purpose in everything and He will not allow anything I can't cope with.

When I look back at my life now, I can see a better and complete picture of my life and understand some things that happened and the time when they happened. I can say without a shadow of doubt that Isaiah 1:19 has become true in my life:

> *"If you are willing and obedient, you will eat the good things of the land."*

Also, I can say with absolute confidence and with my heart full of gratitude that I have reached THE BEST FOR LIFE.

Never lose hope but stand firm and look at what God is doing. Our Father God always wants the best for us and will never allow us to go through anything we cannot endure.

GOD'S ESSENCE IS LOVE!

FEEL FREE TO CONTACT ME

I hope you have been blessed reading this book as much as I have been when I was writing it.

I pray that this book has helped you to understand more about purpose and pai and that you feel encouraged to trust God completely.

I am passionate about sharing what God did and is still doing in my life, and I believe that He can do the same thing for your life. God wants us to live a fulfilled life.

If you feel that you would like more help in finding God's purpose for your life, please feel free to contact me.

I would also like to hear from you, what you think about this book and how you felt it has helped you when you were reading it.

You can connect with me on:

silesiagons@hotmail.com

Instagram: @Martin-Silesia Brown

I would love to hear from my readers.

REVIEW REQUEST

If you enjoyed this book, could you please leave a positive review about it on Amazon? I would really appreciate it if you take your time to help me. My heart will be filled with gratitude and my thoughts will be with you.

My wedding in Brazil

My civil wedding in Yates-UK

My wedding in Bolton-UK

My children and I Joao-Lucas, Maisie and Mia

My girls, Maisie and Mia when they were baby at the NICU and a year ago.

Printed in Great Britain
by Amazon

70297362R00072